THE TEACHING OF JESUS

CONCERNING

THE KINGDOM OF GOD

AND THE CHURCH

GEERHARDUS VOS, PH.D., D. D.

Fontes Press

FONTES PRESS

www.fontespress.com

CONTENTS

FOREWARD TO THE FONTES EDITION

We are pleased to offer this reprint of this useful and still-insightful exposition of the "kingdom-idea" by Geerhardus Vos. We are also thankful to Danny Olinger for providing the introduction, which so ably places Vos's person and ideas in their historical context, and details the academic responses to this book, originally published in 1903.

This edition remains unchanged with some formatting changes. The Scripture citations have been updated from Roman numerals (1 Cor xv 3) to standard modern format (1 Cor 15:3) for ease of reading. Citations have also been moved inside parentheses in accord with modern practice, whereas Vos would simply place them after a comma. A few words whose spelling is antiquated have been modernized. Otherwise, there are no further changes. The Scripture index has been reworked, since the original missed many references and the page numbers differ.

May this exposition of the Kingdom continue to equip a generation to understand Jesus' message and heed his call to "repent and believe in the gospel" (Mark 1:15) and to "seek first the kingdom of God and his righteousness" (Matt 6:33).

INTRODUCTION

GEERHARDUS VOS: FAMILY LIFE, THE KINGDOM OF GOD, AND THE CHURCH

DANNY E. OLINGER

After nine years of teaching at Princeton Seminary, Geerhardus Vos had settled into the rhythm of a quiet professorial life. According to Princeton historian David Calhoun, by 1902, "Dr. Vos's fine features, slightly stooped figure, and quiet dignity were a familiar sight to his fellow Princetonians."[1] Dwelling at 52 Mercer Street with his beloved wife, Catherine, he worshipped at First Presbyterian Church, taught two or three courses per semester at the seminary, took daily walks with his friend Benjamin Warfield, and wrote numerous reviews and articles. When the school year ended, Geerhardus and Catherine would return to the Grand Rapids

---

[1] David B. Calhoun, *Princeton Seminary, The Majestic Testimony, 1869-1929* (Edinburgh: Banner of Truth, 1996), 2:210.

area for the summer to be near their families.[2]

Change, however, was on the way in that Catherine was expecting. According to her daughter, Marianne, "My mother did not have children for the first nine years of her marriage. She then went to a surgeon in Philadelphia who diagnosed that she needed a slight change in a muscle."[3] After that, the problem was alleviated.

On February 4, 1903, Catherine gave birth to a baby boy, Johannes Geerhardus. The next day the members of the senior class at the seminary presented a baby carriage to the new father and mother. According to the *New York Times*, Dr. Vos expressed his thanksgiving for the gift, and then added "that the donation might have been postponed until tomorrow with great propriety, as the subject of his lecture then would be 'The Fatherhood and the Sonship.'"[4] Geerhardus and Catherine also received other gifts from their friends, most notably a silver collapsible drinking cup from Benjamin and Annie Warfield and a silver porringer from Woodrow and Ellen Wilson.[5]

A little over two years later, Bernardus Hendrik was born on April, 19, 1905. Marianne Catherine was born on December 7, 1906, and the last child, Geerhardus Jr., was born on March 7, 1911. As the Vos family was growing, Geerhardus and Catherine purchased a summer home in Roaring Branch, Pennsylvania, north of the city of Williamsport.

After obtaining the house in 1906, they purchased thirteen acres of land between 1908 and 1910 directly outside of Roaring

[2] Interview, Marianne Vos Radius by Charles G. Dennison, February 27, 1992, at the Raybrook Assisted Living Center in Grand Rapids, Michigan, archives of the Orthodox Presbyterian Church.

[3] Ibid.

[4] February 6, 1903, *New York Times*, in *The Letters of Geerhardus Vos*, ed. James T. Dennison Jr. (Philipsburg, NJ: P&R, 2005), 43.

[5] Email, Raymond Vos to Danny Olinger, December 12, 2016.

Branch. Once the land was acquired, they raised the house on rollers and had it moved to the new location with its clear view of the town and the mountains in the background.

After Christmas, Catherine would order the food supplies and clothes for the summer from the Sears Roebuck catalog and have them sent directly to Roaring Branch. Once the school year for the children ended, Catherine and the children would typically travel by train one hundred miles west to Roaring Branch ahead of Geerhardus. As the rest of the family unpacked and set the home up for the summer, Geerhardus would slowly make his way to Roaring Branch by car stopping at hotels with his books in tow. He would read and write and then journey to the next town and the next hotel.[6]

Once the whole family was in Roaring Branch, there was a pattern to the days. A mile walk to the post office in the morning and then again in the evening to pick up any mail. Geerhardus read literature to the entire family situated on the front porch. Catherine read Scripture with a running commentary (which would in time would become the basis of her book, *The Child's Story Bible*), and then Geerhardus prayed. The family would worship on the Lord's Day at the Methodist Church, the only church in town. So beloved was this summer retreat, that when Catherine and Geerhardus Vos died, they would not be buried in Grand Rapids or Princeton, but in Griffin Cemetery in Roaring Branch.

The routine of the family when it returned to Princeton at the end of the summer was geared around the seminary. The Warfields at 74 Mercer Street lived a few houses down from the Vos's home at 52 Mercer Street. Catherine and Marianne would

---

[6] Charles G. Dennison, taped comments to Vos Monday Group, meeting in Sewickley, Pennsylvania, July 21, 1996, archives of the Orthodox Presbyterian Church.

visit Anne Warfield for tea. Once when Marianne had a birthday party and wanted to dress up, Mrs. Warfield loaned her a beautiful shawl.[7]

Geerhardus and Benjamin Warfield would take a daily walk at noon.[8] But, it was not just Warfield who Vos walked with on Mercer Street. J. Gresham Machen, an avid walker himself, would take strolls with Vos, as would other Princeton professors. Also accompanying Vos on his walks would be one of the family dogs. His daughter Marianne described the scene.

> He was fond of dogs. We always had a little dog and a big dog, a dog about the size of a collie, and a little dog. I often remember him walking up and down the street with Machen and some of his other colleagues at Princeton swinging a cane in one hand and a dog following his footsteps as he walked back and forth.[9]

Geerhardus and Catherine were also known for their hospitality, particularly to Dutch friends.[10] Their guests were invited to participate in the family time of Bible reading and prayer.[11] The learning of the Westminster Shorter Catechism in English was emphasized with the children, although there were periods of time in the Vos household when German was the dominant language spoken.[12] If any of the children were

---

[7] Interview, Marianne Radius, archives of the Orthodox Presbyterian Church.

[8] Calhoun, *Princeton Seminary*, 210.

[9] Interview, Marianne Radius, archives of the Orthodox Presbyterian Church.

[10] George Harinck, "Vos as an Introducer of Kuyper in America," in *The Dutch–American Experience*, ed. Hans Krabbendam and Larry J. Wagenaar (Amsterdam: VU Uitgeverij), 244.

[11] Calhoun, *Princeton Seminary*, 210.

[12] Marianne recalled, "For two years we had German governesses, and

puzzled about anything in the Bible or in the Shorter Catechism, they would approach their father after supper in his study. He would listen patiently and attempt to explain to them the meaning of the question and answer.

On the Lord's Day, once Johannes was old enough to lead his siblings, the children would walk to the First Presbyterian Church for Sunday School classes. After Sunday School finished, they would then walk and meet their parents at Princeton's Miller Chapel for worship. Marianne recalled one memorable Lord's Day: "Our parents would already be seated. The students sat in the center. The faculty members had their own assigned seats on the sides. I remember the glorious day when the Stevenson twins had their feet on the pew in the front and the pew in which they and their mother were sitting tipped over."[13]

The Bible Student

In addition to experiencing the dynamics of family life, and settling into his second decade teaching at Princeton, Vos started publishing theological articles that were more accessible to the general public. The accessibility was due mainly to the fact that he kept his analysis of critical viewpoints to a minimum and focused on the exegesis of texts. Six such articles, the majority around 2,500–3,000 words in length, appeared in the newly created *The Bible Student* from 1900–1903. Edited by William McPheeters, professor of Old Testament at Columbia Theological Seminary, and co-edited by

---

we spoke nothing but German in the house." Interview, Marianne Radius. Interestingly, according to George Harinck, once Geerhardus was at Princeton, he hardly spoke Dutch anymore. Harinck, "Vos as an Introducer of Kuyper," 244.

[13] Ibid. In 1914, J. Ross Stevenson became the second president of Princeton Seminary.

Warfield, George Purves, and John Davis of Princeton Seminary, *The Bible Student* was dedicated to promoting traditional biblical doctrines. The articles not only marked a transition for Vos in style, but also signaled the themes that he would develop in his major articles and books. This was most readily seen in Vos's first two *Bible Student* articles, "The Ministry of John the Baptist"[14] and "The Kingdom of God."[15]

In both, Vos presented a redemptive-historical look at the doctrine of the kingdom of God. In examining the role of John the Baptist, Vos exegeted the meaning Jesus's statement in Matthew 11:11 (KJV), "Verily I say unto you, among them that are born of women there hath not risen a greater than John the Baptist: notwithstanding he that is least in the kingdom of heaven is greater than he." Here Jesus declared that John was outside of the New Testament realization of the kingdom of heaven that had inaugurated by Jesus himself. By this, Jesus did not mean that John was not a believer in the Old Testament sense. Rather, John did not share in far greater blessings of the new covenant. Vos explained, "He that is lesser in the kingdom of heaven, i.e., occupies a relatively lower place than John under the Old Testament, is nevertheless absolutely greater than John, because the kingdom itself is far superior to the typical stage of the theocracy."[16]

Although standing outside the kingdom, John understood the great principle on which the kingdom was built, self-denial

---

[14] Geerhardus Vos, "The Ministry of John the Baptist," in *The Bible Student* 1 (1900): 26–32. Reprinted in *Redemptive History and Biblical Interpretation*, ed. Richard B. Gaffin Jr. (Phillipsburg, NJ: P&R, 1980), 299–303.

[15] Geerhardus Vos, "The Kingdom of God," in *The Bible Student* 1 (1900): 282–89, 328–35. Reprinted in *Redemptive History and Biblical Interpretation*, ed. Richard B. Gaffin Jr. (Phillipsburg, NJ: P&R, 1980), 304–316.

[16] Vos, "Ministry of John the Baptist," 300.

and service. John believed that "He (Jesus) must increase, I must decrease" (John 3:30). Consequently, when John was in prison and expressed doubts, Jesus took pains to defend him. Vos commented, "There is to us something unspeakably touching in this loyal gratitude to a faithful servant on the part of Him who had Himself come to serve all others."[17]

In "The Ministry of John the Baptist" Vos examined the *formal* questions that accompanied the conception of the Kingdom of God in looking at the ministry of John the Baptist. He then turned in "The Kingdom of God" to answering *material* questions.[18] According to Vos, the content of the doctrine of the kingdom of God represented the whole sum and substance of the teaching of Jesus. Jesus taught that with his arrival the kingdom of God was both a present and future reality. As the kingdom was centered in God himself and in his glory, Jesus represented the kingdom as the highest object after which men are to strive.

Vos followed the two articles with two reviews that revealed that he was not entirely satisfied with what others were teaching on the subject of the kingdom of God. The first was a review of Wilhelm Lütgert's *Das Reich Gottes nach den synoptischen Evangelien*.[19] Lütgert believed that the kingdom

---

[17] Ibid., 303.

[18] In "The Kingdom of God," Vos wrote, "In a previous article we endeavored to discuss some of the formal questions that cluster around the conception of the kingdom of God. We must now look for a moment at the content of the idea from a material point of view" (310).

[19] Geerhardus Vos, *review of Das Reich Gottes nach den synoptischen Evangelisn*, by W. Lütgert, *Presbyterian and Reformed Review* 11:171–74. Wilhelm Lütgert (1867–1937) was professor of New Testament at Griefswald. He would move to the University of Halle in 1901 and serve there as professor of Systematic Theology. In 1929 he succeeded Reinhold Seeberg as the chairman of Systematic Theology at the University of Berlin.

was entirely present. According to Vos, this one-sided insistence that the kingdom was wholly present blinded Lütgert to the fact that the kingdom of God is both a reign and a realm.

In his review of Paul Wernle's *Die Reichsgotteshoffnung in den altesten Christlichen dokumenten und bei Jesus*,[20] Vos contended that Wernle's eschatological view of the kingdom of God errored in the other direction. Wernle altered the sayings of Jesus in order to argue against a present kingdom. He also denied that righteousness was a part of the conception of the kingdom. For Vos the result was the worst of all possibilities, a kingdom that did not consist in righteousness or communion with God prior to the last day.

It was evident from the article and the two reviews that Vos did not agree with the doctrine of the kingdom being put forth in his day. On the one hand, the immanent school (Lütgert) taught that the kingdom of God was entirely present and disregarded the supernatural work of God. On the other hand, the eschatological school (Wernle) posited that the kingdom of God was entirely future and weakened the Bible's authority in the realm of ethics. What was needed was a redemptive-historical exegesis of the Lord's doctrine of the kingdom of God

---

Dietrich Bonhoeffer would serve as Lütgert's academic assistant at Berlin, and Lütgert as Bonhoeffer's advisor would help Bonhoeffer publish his postdoctoral dissertation, *Act and Being*.

[20] Geerhardus Vos, review of *Die Reichsgotteshoffnung in den altesten christlichen Dokumenten und bei Jesus*, by Paul Wernle, *Princeton Theological Review* 1:298–303. Paul Wernle (1872-1939), professor of New Testament Studies at the University of Basel, was the most influential Swiss theologian of the early twentieth century. A History of Religions proponent, Wernle befriended and mentored Karl Barth for the period leading up to World War I. Richard Burnett has argued that Barth had no modern theologian more in view when writing his commentaries on Romans than Wernle. See, Richard Burnett, *Karl Barth's Theological Exegesis* (Grand Rapids, MI: Eerdmans), 136.

without the overreach of modern theology.

The Teaching of Jesus Concerning the Kingdom of God and the Church

When Vos's 1903 book *The Teaching of Jesus Regarding the Kingdom of God and the Church* appeared, it was clear that he had used his previously published material. The "Kingdom of God" article provided the outline and bulk of the content for the first five chapters of the book, the sentences slightly changed and paragraphs rearranged. The remaining chapters of the book, prior to the concluding "Recapitulation" chapter, exegetically confronted the liberal conceptions regarding the essence of the kingdom that he had challenged in the reviews.[21]

In the self-effacing fashion that matched his personality, Vos did not include a preface, forward, or acknowledgements in the book. The book began with Chapter 1, "Introductory," but the chapter did not partake of the nature of a typical introduction. More accurately, it should have been labelled "The Public Ministry of Jesus," for that was the topic that Vos immediately addressed from the start. Vos noted that Jesus declared the kingdom of God was at hand. The main purpose of Jesus's mission consisted in the preaching of the good news of the kingdom of God.[22]

---

[21] Although Vos's *Reformed Dogmatics* included a section on the relationship of the kingdom of heaven and the church, he did not repeat the same line of argumentation in *The Teaching of Jesus Regarding the Kingdom of God and the Church*. See, "Chapter One: Essence," and "Chapter Two: Organization, Discipline, Offices," in Geerhardus Vos, *Reformed Dogmatics*, vol. 5, *Ecclesiology, the Means of Grace, Eschatology*, trans. and ed. Richard B. Gaffin Jr. with Kim Batteau and Allan Janssen (Bellingham, WA: Lexham, 2016), 3–74.

[22] Page 1 below.

Still, Vos maintained that God himself, and not the kingdom, occupied the highest place in the teaching of Jesus. All that salvation contained flowed from the nature of God and served the glory of God. This is why Jesus did not speak of the "kingdom," but spoke of the "kingdom of God" or "the kingdom of heaven."

But, in appropriating for himself the function of bringing in the kingdom and in laying claim to the Messianic dignity promised in the Old Testament, Jesus knew himself as both the goal of history and the servant of history. The entire historic movement converged upon and terminated in him.

Still, Jesus did not speak of the kingdom of God as previously existing. Vos explained, "To [Jesus's] mind [the kingdom] involved such altogether new forces and unparalleled blessings, that all relative and provisional forms previously assumed by the work of God on earth seemed by comparison unworthy of the name."[23] For Judaism, the divine rule was equivalent to the sovereignty of the law. Jesus did not exclude this, but he "knew of a much larger sphere in which God would through saving acts exercise his glorious prerogatives of kingship on a scale and in a manner unknown before."[24]

While the Jewish habit to substitute "heaven" for "God" was meant to emphasize God's unapproachable majesty, Vos believed such a mode of speech endangered "what must ever be the essence of religion, a true communion between God and man."[25] Jesus used "kingdom of heaven" to awaken in his disciples a sense of the mysterious, supernatural character of heaven, that realm of absolute perfection and grandeur, and for them to value above all the new order of things. "If the king be

---

[23] Page 9 below.
[24] Page 11 below.
[25] Page 17 below.

one who concentrates in himself all the glory of heaven, what must his kingdom be?"[26]

Vos then laid out what the church historically had believed concerning the coming of the kingdom.

> The kingdom, it was believed, comes when the gospel is spread, hearts are changed, sin and error overcome, righteousness cultivated, a living communion with God established. In this sense the kingdom began its coming when Jesus entered upon his public ministry, his work upon earth, including his death, was part of its realization, the disciples were in it, the whole subsequent history of the church is the history of its gradual extension, we ourselves can act our part in its onward movement and are members of it as a present organization.[27]

This view, Vos maintained, was under attack in Christendom as unhistorical. Jesus was only a man, and no man could bring in the kingdom. God would bring in the kingdom in a great world-crisis, one that Jesus expected in his lifetime.

Both views held that Jesus associated the coming of the kingdom in its final absolute sense with the end of the world. Where the views differed was whether Jesus's spiritual labors brought about the beginning of the kingdom. How one decided this question had the gravest consequences, for it involved the question of the infallibility of Jesus's teaching. If he expected only one coming of the kingdom to happen within his lifetime, then there is no escape from the conclusion that he was mistaken.[28]

---

[26] Page 18 below.

[27] Page 21 below.

[28] Vos did not name Albert Schweitzer (1875–1965) directly, but it is unmistakable that he was contrasting Schweitzer's view of the kingdom

According to Vos, the modern views necessitated ascribing to the Scripture an unhistorical representation of what Jesus actually taught. For those who held to the trustworthiness of the Gospel accounts, there was no doubt that Jesus's Messianic labor ushered in the kingdom prior to the last day.

Further, as Jesus distinguished his Messianic activity on earth in humility and his Messianic activity from the throne of glory, he also distinguished two different aspects, the immanent and the eschatological, of the kingdom of God. It followed that "the ancient theological distinction between a kingdom of grace and a kingdom of glory is infelicitous."[29]

Vos also believed that the kingdom of God was not a means to an end apart from man's glorifying and enjoying God. This was seen in a proper understanding of the theocracy in the Old Covenant. The theocracy's primary purpose was "to reflect the eternal laws of religious intercourse between God and man as they will exist in the consummate life at the end."[30] This focus on the procuring of life and communion with God is why Jesus did not view the kingdom conflict as being Israel versus Rome. The true conflict is the kingdom of God versus the kingdom of Satan.

Although the glory of God, not man's welfare, was the

---

with the traditional understanding of the kingdom throughout this section. For an analysis of Schweitzer's views, see Robert Strimple's *The Modern Search for the Real Jesus* (Phillipsburg, NJ: P&R, 1995).

[29] Page 33. Although Vos did not make direct reference to Westminster Shorter Question and Answer 102, it is clear that he had this in view with this statement. Q. 102. *What do we pray for in the second petition?* A. In the second petition which is, *Thy kingdom come*, we pray that Satan's kingdom may be destroyed; and that the kingdom of grace may be advanced, ourselves and others brought into it, and kept in it; and that the kingdom of glory may be hastened.

[30] Page 44 below.

supreme concern of the kingdom, this did not mean that blessing and happiness were found apart from the kingdom. Kingdom members enjoy the blessedness of union and communion with the living God, which brings happiness and joy in this life. Such communion is both a gift from Jesus and the life to which the Christian aspires. The reward bears an organic relation to the conduct it intends to crown.

In discussing the relationship of the kingdom of God to the church, Vos exegeted Matthew 16:18–19. The church, formed by Jesus and under his rule, is the new congregation of God as it confesses Jesus in the midst of persecution. It takes the place of the old congregation of Israel that refused to recognize Jesus as Messiah.

The church in a sense can rightly be called the kingdom. It is another question altogether whether the kingdom at all times can be identified with the church. The church is the form that the kingdom assumes because of the death and resurrection of Jesus Christ. Through the Messianic acts of Jesus and an influx of supernatural power, the church has within it the presence of the Spirit, which is the power of the age to come.

Jesus identified the invisible church and the kingdom. But, the kingdom-life that exists in the invisible church must find a parallel expression in the kingdom-organism of the visible church. The visible church is not the only expression of the kingdom.

Realizing that he was qualifying many things regarding the relationship of the kingdom of God to the church, Vos said that two things may be safely affirmed. On the one hand, the supremacy of God in all things is the foundation on which the Lord's doctrine of the kingdom is founded. This meant that Jesus saw every normal and legitimate province of life as intended to form part of God's kingdom. On the other hand,

Jesus did not believe that all of the spheres of life should be subject to the visible church in order to achieve this result.

Vos maintained that repentance and faith are prerequisites for entrance into the kingdom of God. Jesus cried out, "Repent, for the kingdom of heaven is at hand" (Matt. 4:17). This demand resulted from the nature of the kingdom. "Repentance and faith are simply the two main aspects of the kingdom, righteousness and the saving grace of God, translated into terms of subjective human experience."[31] Repentance and righteousness do not earn the benefits of the kingdom, but they accompany the kingdom in such a way that through them the benefits of the kingdom come to believers.

The Lord's teaching on repentance engages the entire person, intellect, will and affections. It includes man's relationship to God, both religious and moral. Jesus's conception of repentance is even wide enough to include faith. No neutrality or indifference exists when it comes to repentance. There is either love or hatred for God, or love or hatred for the world. He who repents turns from love and service of the world to the love and service of God.

The total supremacy of God in one's life as a controlling principle is why Jesus requires that his disciples renounce all earthly relations and possessions that might take God's place. This does not mean, however, that the believer must abandon all relations and possessions in this life. What must be destroyed is the attachment of the soul to relations and possessions as the highest good. The demand for sacrifice presupposes that what is renounced forms an obstacle to the absolute devotion of God.

Vos ended the book with a summary chapter entitled "Recapitulation." In it, he listed seven principles from Jesus's

---

[31] Page 87 below.

teaching on the kingdom of God and the church.[32]

1. There is no separation between the Old Testament work of God and Jesus's work. The two constitute a single body of supernatural revelation and redemption.

Here Vos challenged both fundamentalist and modernist interpretations concerning the kingdom. On the fundamentalist side, chiliasm did not acknowledge that old and new constitute one body of supernatural revelation and redemption. On the critical side, modernists denied that Jesus himself was self-conscious of the unity that existed between the Old Testament promise and his fulfillment. For Vos, the Scriptures testified and the Reformed Faith affirmed the unity between the promises of God in the Old Testament and Jesus' fulfillment of the promises in the New Testament.

2. The doctrine of the kingdom does not teach that Christianity is a mere matter of subjective ideas or experiences. Rather, it teaches that the kingdom is related to a great system of objective, supernatural facts and transactions.

With the second principle, Vos opposed the liberal theological belief that the doctrine of the kingdom illustrated that Christianity was primary a subjective religion based on experience. Vos believed that the doctrine of the kingdom mandated that Christianity was an objective religion based on the supernatural work of God in history. There is a subjective element to Christianity, but without the objective work of God

---

[32] Pages 98–99 below.

grounding it, there is no basis for faith.

3. The kingdom-conception teaches that all of life is subservient to the glory of God. This is why the kingdom-conception is the most profoundly religious of all biblical conceptions.

The third principle was Vos's acknowledgment that the Reformed faith had understood the Scriptures and the doctrine of the kingdom correctly when it confessed that man's chief end was to glorify God and to enjoy him forever. The kingdom of God is an otherworldly reign and realm in which God and his glory is all-important.

4. The message the kingdom imparts to Christianity is that salvation is by the power and grace of God. This principle is connected to the necessity of faith.

Having affirmed the Reformed position in principle three, Vos pivoted in the fourth principle to show the errors of liberalism, Arminianism and Roman Catholicism concerning the relationship between the kingdom and salvation. Salvation is not through the effort of man, but the work of God alone.

5. Jesus's doctrine of the kingdom upholds the primacy of the spiritual over the physical. The ultimate realities of the invisible world, to which everything else is subordinate, form the essence of the kingdom. This principle is connected to the demand for repentance.

The unseen realities of heaven constitute the essence of the kingdom of God. Liberalism tied the ethical solely to this world, which left no place for biblical faith and repentance. There is an ethical dimension to the kingdom, but it has to do with repentance from sin and faith in Christ.

6. The form which the kingdom takes in the church shows it to be inseparably related to the person and work of Jesus himself.

In the sixth principle, Vos stated without reservation or qualification that Jesus Christ stands central to the church. Without Christ's historical person and work, there is no Christianity worth proclaiming. To remove Christ as Savior from his church would be to remove the church's reason for existence because upon Christ everything depends.

7. The concept of the kingdom of God implies the subjection of the entire range of human life to the ends of religion. The kingdom reminds us of the absoluteness, the pervasiveness, the unrestricted dominion, which of right belongs to all true religion. It proclaims that religion, and religion alone, can act as the supreme unifying, centralizing factor in the life of man, as that which binds all together and perfects all by leading it to its final goal in the service of God.

The kingdom of God in Jesus's teaching informs the believer's life in total. Complete devotion to God is demanded in everything that is done. But, such a service, a giving of oneself for the living God, is the only one that gives meaning and value to life.

Reviews

In a turn that had to be amusing to some, and perhaps an indication of Vos's quiet service at Princeton, Vos himself reviewed *The Kingdom of God and the Church* in the *Presbyterian and Reformed Review*. Vos-the-reviewer explained that the aim of Vos-the-author was to produce a popular and yet not too elementary discussion from the biblico-theological point of view on Jesus's doctrine of the kingdom. Vos proceeded to summarize the headings of the chapters without adding any insights other than the topics covered. He ended the review by stating that the book had an index and large type.[33]

In what would be typical of the writings of Vos, later generations of Reformed theologians would rescue *The Kingdom of God and the Church* from obscurity. In particular, Vos's students at Princeton who went on to teach at Westminister Theological Seminary, John Murray, Ned B. Stonehouse, and Cornelius Van Til, each praised the book in print and in their classes. When the book was reprinted in 1951, Murray reviewed it in the *Westminster Theological Journal*.[34]

---

[33] In many ways Vos's statement in his *Biblical Theology* provided more of a summary of *The Kingdom of God and the Church* than his review did. Vos wrote, "The kingdom is in its intent an instrument of redemption as well as the embodiment of the blessedness of Israel. To it the Messianic expectations attach themselves. It is a serious mistake to conceive of the kingdom as something accidentally arrived at, and merely tolerated for a time at the expense of democracy. The thing was too large and deep to have aught of the unessential and dispensable about it. It touches, through the kingship of Christ, the very acme and perfection of the Biblical religion." Geerhardus Vos, *Biblical Theology* (Grand Rapids, MI: Eerdmans, 1985), 185–86.

[34] John Murray, review of *The Teaching of Jesus Concerning the Kingdom and the Church*, by Geerhardus Vos, *Westminster Theological Journal* 14:230–31.

Murray commented that it had been nearly half a century since the book was first published, but that the volume was far from obsolete. He said:

> It is one of those books which have permanent value, for it is a masterful presentation of the teaching of Jesus as presented in the four Gospels. It exhibits the profound and accurate scholarship which was characteristic of all Dr. Vos's work and it is also written in a style which is not as heavy as that of some of the other volumes of Dr. Vos's pen. It is splendid to have this new edition of so notable a work.[35]

Murray believed, however, that Vos would be disappointed with the one change that the Wm. B. Eerdmans Publishing Company had made in republishing the book, the change of the title of the book from *The Teaching of Jesus Concerning the Kingdom of God and the Church* to *The Teaching of Jesus Concerning the Kingdom and the Church*. "On one thing Dr. Vos was insistent–we not speak of the Kingdom but of the Kingdom of God. That emphasis was pivotal in Vos's thought."[36]

Still, Murray was thankful that the book would be receiving a new audience. He finished, "Vos provides us with a biblico-theological study which supplies us with the conceptions which must guide and govern our thinking if we are to be faithful to him who went preaching the kingdom of God."[37]

In the same issue of the *Westminster Theological Journal*, Ned B. Stonehouse reviewed the Dutch edition of Herman Ridderbos's *The Coming of the Kingdom*.[38] In what he considered

---

[35] Ibid.

[36] Ibid.

[37] Ibid., 231.

[38] Ned B. Stonehouse, Review of *De Komst van het Koninkrijk,* by H. N. Ridderbos, *Westminster Theological Journal* 14:160.

high praise, Stonehouse wrote that Ridderbos's volume "may advantageously be compared with that of Geerhardus Vos on *The Teaching of Jesus concerning the Kingdom of God and the Church.*"[39] Stonehouse continued:

> Broadly speaking the same conception of the significance and scope of the kingdom of God appears in both volumes, which is rather remarkable in view of the consideration that Vos's treatise evidently was not known to Ridderbos at the time that he wrote the work. If one takes in account, however, the fact that Ridderbos like Vos stands squarely in the stream of the Reformed tradition, sharing its convictions and insights, and is also a scholar of wide learning and rare exegetical skill, the larger measure of agreement will not appear as a bare coincidence. It is refreshing, nevertheless, to receive a new reminder that after fifty years Vos's fundamental perspectives and conclusions are by no means outdated.[40]

Even when he then turned to talking about the advantages of having Ridderbos's *Coming of the Kingdom* in print, Stonehouse could not help himself but turn back to Vos's contribution. Stonehouse said that Ribberbos had provided a book on the kingdom of God with a far greater scope, but "brevity in the hands of a precise thinker like Vos is not necessarily a serious liability, and my impression is that his little book will long remain a classic because of its masterful analysis and formulation of various aspects of the subject."[41] Stonehouse's recommendation was to keep Ridderbos's volume close as a reference tool continually to be consulted, but to read

---

[39] Ibid.
[40] Ibid.
[41] Ibid.

Vos's book at least once a year.[42]

Van Til leaned heavily upon Vos when talking about the kingdom of God in his book *Christian Theistic Ethics.* In it Van Til declared the kingdom of God "is a gift of free grace to man and that therefore the *summum bonum* is a free gift to man."[43] According to Van Til, "Vos has worked this out beautifully in his little book, *Concerning the Kingdom of God and the Church.* The kingdom of God is not realized by self-righteousness but by the righteousness of God, which must be given to men."[44]

In detailing how the kingdom of God was both a present reality and goal, Van Til again turned to Vos. "The kingdom of God is a present reality. We have entered into it. But it is also that for the realization of which we daily strive. Dr. Vos has made this two-fold aspect of the kingdom abundantly clear on the basis of the teaching of Jesus."[45]

In explaining how righteousness, holiness, and blessedness belong together in the kingdom of God, Van Til referenced Vos's

---

[42]Ibid. Richard B. Gaffin, Jr., a student of Stonehouse in the late 1950s at Westminster Seminary, testifies that Stonehouse declared more than once in the classroom that every minister of the gospel should read Vos's *Kingdom of God and the Church* annually. Email to author, March 10, 2017.

[43] Cornelius Van Til, *Christian Theistic Ethics* (Phillipsburg, NJ: P&R, 1980), 78.

[44] Ibid.

[45] Ibid., 90. Richard Gaffin Jr. echoes Vos and Van Til in his article, "The Bible and the Whole Counsel of God," which honored Vos's son, Johannes. Gaffin wrote, "The kingdom of God is the fundamental and all-encompassing category. Accordingly, the gospel (of God's grace) is the gospel of the kingdom and its coming. Repentance and faith are the primary blessings of the kingdom. Worked by the grace of God, they are the way of entrance into and continuance in the kingdom of God." See, Richard B. Gaffin, Jr., "The Bible and the Whole Counsel of God," in *The Book of Books: Essays on the Scriptures in Honor of Johannes G. Vos*, ed. John H. White (Phillipsburg, NJ: P&R, 1978), 21.

Kingdom of God and the Church once more. Van Til wrote:

> Dr. Vos makes plain that there is a two-fold aspect to Jesus' teaching of the kingdom. Righteousness and conversion have to do with the present aspect of the kingdom, and blessedness primarily with the future aspect of the kingdom. Apart from the fact that those who are in the kingdom are now blessed, in the sense that they know themselves to be heirs of God, their actual and complete blessedness lies in the future. They cannot be completely blessed till all of sin and all of the results of sin are done away. Hence they cannot be perfectly blessed till their own souls are perfectly and permanently cleansed from the last remnant of sin . . . In short, they cannot be fully blessed till "the regeneration of all things."[46]

Orthodox Presbyterian historian Charles Dennison, a student of Van Til and Gaffin at Westminster, also highly praised the book. In particular, he observed that Vos's concluding chapter, "Recapitulation," was no summary in the ordinary sense. In summarizing Vos's seven principles, Dennison said, "For Vos, Jesus' theological method rises first of all from the historical reality of God's interaction with this world. This historical reality involves the historical unity of God's Old Testament work and Jesus' labors recorded in the gospels."[47]

Dennison continued, "Indispensable to Jesus' theology is his identity as Savior, a fact from which his church cannot separate itself and still be called the church. For Jesus to be Savior, in his theology of the kingdom, means the essential message of faith

---

[46] Ibid., 121.

[47] Manuscript of comments made to Vos Monday study group in Sewickley, Pennsylvania, September 21, 1998. See, *A Geerhardus Vos Anthology*, ed. Danny E. Olinger (Phillipsburg, NJ: P&R, 2004), 27.

and repentance to those who would enter the kingdom."[48] In Dennison's judgment, Vos had rightly understood the essence of the kingdom. "The essence of the kingdom is understood in terms of salvation for another world, righteousness for that world, and blessedness intimately, in it."[49]

Dennison questioned, however, if the book reflected an "idealism" on Vos's part that he moved away from in his more mature writings.[50] Vos would declare later in his *Pauline Eschatology* that "the historical was first, then the theological."[51] The coming of the kingdom of God is a great event, not an ideal.

Charles Dennison's older brother, James T. Dennison Jr., focused on Vos's opposition to nineteenth-century liberal views and early twentieth-century apocalyptic views of the kingdom of God. These views desupernaturalized the kingdom in contrast to Jesus's proclamation. Dennison also noted that Vos emphasized the eschatological nature of the kingdom. He wrote, "The 'now' and 'not yet' (or the two ages) of Jesus' kingdom proclamation surpass Judaism with its nationalistic, political, sensual kingdom hopes. The presence and future of the kingdom that Jesus brings contravenes classic liberalism that immanentizes the eschaton."[52]

Although very appreciative of Vos's contributions as a whole, George Eldon Ladd believed that Vos had erred in his identification of the kingdom and the church when interpreting Matthew 16:18–19.[53] Ladd wrote, "Vos presses metaphorical

---

[48] Ibid.

[49] Ibid.

[50] Charles Dennison, comments made on December 15, 1997, at the "Vos Monday" gathering in Sewickley, Pennsylvania.

[51] Geerhardus Vos, *The Pauline Eschatology* (Philipsburg, NJ: Presbyterian and Reformed, 1986), 41.

[52] Dennison, "The Life of Geerhardus Vos," 55.

[53] Matthew 16:18–19 (KJV), "And I say also unto thee, That thou art Peter,

language too far when he insists that this identification must be made because the first part of the saying speaks of the founding of the house and the second part sees the same house complete with doors and keys."[54] Ladd concluded that "Vos confidently affirms the church is the kingdom."[55]

According to Ladd, a better understanding of the text is that there exists an inseparable relationship, but not an identity. The many sayings about entering into the kingdom are not the same as entering into the church.

A closer reading of the context from which Ladd pulled the quote indicates that Vos's affirmation was more carefully nuanced that Ladd reported. Vos argued that when Jesus declared that Peter had been given the keys of the kingdom to bind and loose on earth, that declaration must be understood in light of the earlier declaration regarding Peter as the foundation rock. Vos said, "First the house is represented as in process of building, and Peter as the foundation, then the same house appears as completed and Peter as invested with the keys for administering its affairs."[56] This is followed by the statement that Ladd quoted and the statement that he paraphrased, "It is plainly excluded that the house should mean one thing in the first statement and another in the second. It must be possible, this much we may confidently affirm, to call the church the

---

and upon this rock I will build my church; and the gates of hell shall not prevail against it. And I will give unto thee the keys of the kingdom of heaven: and whatsoever thou shalt bind on earth shall be bound in heaven: and whatsoever thou shalt loose on earth shall be loosed in heaven."

[54] George Eldon Ladd, *The Presence of the Future* (Grand Rapids, MI: Eerdmans, 1984), 263–264. Ladd repeats the same statement verbatim in *A Theology of the New Testament* (Grand Rapids, MI: Eerdmans, 1991), 112.

[55] Ladd, *The Presence of the Future*, 264, and *A Theology of the New Testament*, 112.

[56] Page 77 below.

kingdom."[57] What Ladd does not add is Vos's next statement, "It is another question, to which we shall presently revert, whether the kingdom can under all circumstances be identified with the church."[58]

For Vos, the church was in possession of the powers of the world to come. The kingdom-life which existed in the invisible sphere found expression in the kingdom-organism of the visible church. But, it did not necessarily follow that the outward expression of the kingdom was found only in the visible church. He said, "While it is proper to separate between the visible church and such things as the Christian state, Christian art, Christian science, etc., these things, if they truly belong to the kingdom of God, grow up out of the regenerated life of the invisible church."[59] The question would become whether Vos maintained this view of the church and culture in his more mature biblical-theological writings.

[57] Page 77 below.
[58] Page 77 below.
[59] Page 84 below.

CHAPTER 1

INTRODUCTORY

I n the body of our Lord's teaching as recorded in the Gospels the references to the kingdom of God occupy a prominent place. According to the common testimony of the Synoptical Gospels Jesus opened his public ministry in Galilee with the announcement, that the kingdom was at hand, Matt 4:17; Mark 1:15; Luke 4:43. In the last mentioned passage he even declares that the main purpose of his mission consists in the preaching of the good tidings of the kingdom of God. And not only does the conception thus stand significantly at the beginning of our Lord's work, it reappears at the culminating points of his teaching, as in the beatitudes of the Sermon on the Mount and in the kingdom-parables. Its importance will best be felt by considering that the coming of the kingdom is the great event which Jesus connects with his appearance and activity, and that consequently in his teaching, which was so closely dependent on his working, this event must also have a corresponding prominence.

If this be true from Jesus' own standpoint, it is no less true from the standpoint of his disciples. In their life likewise the kingdom of God forms the supreme object of pursuit, and therefore of necessity the theme about which before all other things they need careful instruction. Again, the work of those whom Jesus trained as his special helpers in preaching related chiefly to this same subject, for he speaks of them as scribes made disciples to the kingdom of heaven (Matt 13:52). Better than by mere statistics showing the explicit references to the kingdom in our Lord's discourses can we along the above lines be led to appreciate how large a place the subject of our investigation must have had in his thought.

It might be objected to all this, that in the version which the Fourth Gospel gives of Jesus' teaching, the idea of the kingdom plays a very subordinate role, indeed occurs only twice altogether, viz., John 3:3, 5; 18:36. But this is a feature explainable from the peculiarity of John's Gospel in general. Here the person of Jesus as the Son of God stands in the foreground, and the whole compass of his work is represented as given in and resulting from his person. Salvation according to the discourses preserved in this Gospel is made up of those primal elements into which the being of Christ can be resolved, such as light, life, grace, truth. What the Saviour does is the outcome of what he is. In the Synoptists on the other hand *the work* of Jesus is made central and all-important, and especially during the earlier stages of his ministry his person and personal relation to this work are only so much referred to as the circumstances of the discourse make absolutely necessary.

After all, however, this amounts only to a different mode of viewing the same things: there is no contradiction involved as to their inner essence. In a significant saying uttered even before the beginning of his great Galilean ministry our Lord himself has affirmed the identity of the kingdom with at least one of the conceptions that dominate his teaching according to John, viz., that of life. To Nicodemus he speaks of the mysterious birth of water and the Spirit as the only entrance into the kingdom of God. Now, inasmuch as birth is that process by which one enters into life, and since in the immediately following context life is silently substituted for the kingdom, it is plain that these two are practically equivalent, just as the sphere of truth and the kingdom are equivalent in the other passage, John 18:36. With this accords the fact that in the Synoptical teaching the reverse may occasionally be observed, viz., that life is used interchangeably with the kingdom, cf. Mark 10:17 with 10:23.

While thus recognizing that the kingdom of God has an importance in our Lord's teaching second to that of no other subject, we should not go to the extreme into which some writers have fallen, of finding in it the only theme on which Jesus actually taught, which would imply that all other topics dealt with in his discourses were to his mind but so many corollaries or subdivisions of this one great truth. The modern attempts to make the kingdom of God the organizing center of a theological system have here exerted a misleading influence upon the interpretation of Jesus' teaching. From the fact that the proximate object of his saving work was the realization of the kingdom, the wrong inference has been drawn, that this must have been also the highest category under which he viewed the truth. It is plain that the one does not follow from the other. Salvation with all it contains flows from the nature and subserves the glory of God, and we can clearly perceive that Jesus was accustomed consciously to refer it to this divine source and to subordinate it to this God-centered purpose, cf. John 17:4. He usually spoke not of "the kingdom" absolutely, but of "the kingdom of God" and "the kingdom of heaven," and these names themselves indicate that the place of God in the order of things which they describe is the all-important thing to his mind.

It is only with great artificiality that the various component elements of our Lord's teaching can be subsumed under the one head of the kingdom. If any deduction and systematizing are to be attempted, logic and the indications which we have of our Lord's habit of thought on this point alike require, that not his teaching on the kingdom but that on God shall be given the highest place. The relation observable in the discourses of the Fourth Gospel between the person of Christ and salvation, is also the relation which we may conceive to exist between God and the kingdom. Because God is what he is, the kingdom bears the character and embodies the principles which as a matter of fact belong to it. Even so, however, we should avoid the modern mistake of endeavoring to derive the idea of the kingdom from the conception of the divine fatherhood alone. This derivation expresses an important truth recognized by Jesus himself, when he calls the kingdom a fatherly gift to the disciples (Luke 12:32). But it represents only one side of the truth, for in the kingdom other attributes of God besides his fatherhood find expression. The doctrine of God in its entire fullness alone is capable of furnishing that broader basis on which the structure of his teaching on the kingdom can be built in agreement with Jesus' own mind.

On the other hand, it cannot be denied that in many respects the idea of the kingdom acted in our Lord's thought and teaching as a crystallizing point around which several other elements of truth naturally gathered and grouped themselves in harmonious combination. That the idea of the church, where it emerges in his teaching, is a direct outgrowth of the development of his doctrine of the kingdom, will appear in the sequel. But not only this, also the consummation of the world and the final state of glory were evidently viewed by him in no other light than as the crowning fulfilment of the kingdom-idea. Still further what he taught about righteousness was most closely interlinked in his mind with the truth about the nature of the kingdom. The same may safely be affirmed with reference to the love and grace of God. The great categories of subjective religion, faith and repentance and regeneration, obviously had their place in his thought as answering to certain aspects of the kingdom. Even a subject apparently so remote from the kingdom-idea, in our usual understanding of it, as that of miracles in reality derived for Jesus from the latter the larger part of its meaning. Finally, the kingdom stood in our Lord's mind for a very definite conception concerning the historical relation of his own work and the new order of things introduced by it to the Old Testament. All this can here be stated in general only; our task in the sequel will be to work it out in detail. But what has been said is sufficient to show that there is scarcely an important subject in the rich repertoire of our Lord's teaching with which our study of his disclosures concerning the kingdom of God will not bring us into contact.

CHAPTER 2

THE KINGDOM AND THE OLD TESTAMENT

The first thing to be noticed in Jesus' utterances on our theme is that they clearly presuppose a consciousness on his part of standing with his work on the basis of the revelation of God in the Old Testament. Our Lord occupies historic ground from the outset. From first to last he refers to "the kingdom of God" as a fixed conception with which he takes for granted, his hearers are familiar. In affirming that it is "at hand" he moreover ascribes to it the character of something forming part of that world of prophecy, which moves onward through the ages to its divinely appointed goal of fulfillment. It were utterly out of harmony with this fundamental principle of our Lord's kingdom-gospel to represent him as the founder of a new religion. His work was the realization of what in the ideal form of prophecy had been known and expected ages before. We simply here observe at a peculiarly vital point what underlies as a broad uniform basis his official consciousness everywhere. No array of explicit statements in which he acknowledges his acceptance of the Old Testament Scriptures as the word of God can equal in force this implied subordination of himself and of his work to the one great scheme of which the ancient revelation given to Israel formed the preparatory stage. Indeed in appropriating for himself the function of bringing the kingdom, in laying claim to the Messianic dignity. Jesus seized upon that in the Old Testament which enabled him at one stroke to make its whole historic movement converge upon and terminate in himself. There is in this a unique combination of the most sublime self-consciousness and the most humble submission to the revelation of God in former ages. Jesus knew himself as at once the goal of history and the servant of history.

The Old Testament knows of a kingdom of God as already existing at that time. Apart from the universal reign exercised by God as Creator of all things, Jehovah has his special kingdom in Israel. The classical passage relating to the latter is Exod 19:4–6, from which it appears, that the making of the covenant at Sinai established this relationship. In virtue of it, Jehovah, besides being Israel's God, also acted as Israel's national King. By direct revelation he gave them laws and by his subsequent guidance of their history he made his rule a living reality. Even later, when human kings arose, these had no other rights from the point of view of the legitimate religion than those of the vicegerents of Jehovah. The meaning of this order of things was that in Israel's life all other interests, both public and private, were subordinated to and made a part of religion. Whilst elsewhere religion was a function of the state, here the state became a function of religion. In itself this idea of a kingship exercised by the deity over the entire range of life was not confined to the sphere of special revelation. *Melekh* (מֶ֫לֶךְ), "king," was a common name for the godhead among the Semitic tribes, so that to some extent, the principle of what we call "the theocracy" was known to them. But the relation which they imagined to exist between themselves and their gods was in

Israel alone a matter of actual experience. A most vivid consciousness of this fact pervades the entire Old Testament.

In view of this it creates some surprise at first sight, that Jesus never speaks of the kingdom of God as previously existing. To him the kingdom is throughout something new, now first to be realized. Even of John the Baptist he speaks as not being in the kingdom, because his whole manner of work identified him with the preceding dispensation. The law and the prophets are until John: from that time the gospel of the kingdom of God is preached (Luke 16:16; Matt 11:13). There are only two passages in which the old theocratic order of things might seem to be referred to under the name of the kingdom. In Matt 8:12, Jesus calls the Jews "the sons of the kingdom." But this is probably meant in the sense, that in virtue of the promises they are heirs of the kingdom, not in the sense of their having had the kingdom in actual possession before the coming of Christ. On the same principle we must probably interpret Matt 21:43, where Jesus predicts that the kingdom of God shall be taken away from the Jews and given to a nation bringing forth the fruits thereof, the kingdom being used for the title to the kingdom. Or, if the literal meaning of the words be pressed, it should be remembered, that our Lord spoke them during the later stage of his ministry, at a time when through his labors the kingdom of God in its new and highest sense had been at least incipiently realized.

The only indirect recognition of God's kingship under the Old Testament is found in Matt 5:35, where Jerusalem is called "the city of the great King." When the question is put, how must we explain this restriction of the term by Jesus to the new order of things, the answer cannot of course be sought in any lack of appreciation on his part of the reasons which underlie the opposite usage prevailing in the Old Testament. Nor can the reason have lain in a desire to accommodate himself to the contemporary Jewish conception, for, although the Jews at that time expected the kingdom from the future, they also knew it in another sense as already present with them through the reign of God in the law. The true explanation is undoubtedly to be found in the absolute, ideal character our Lord ascribed to the order of things associated with the name of the kingdom. To his mind it involved such altogether new forces and such unparalleled blessings, that all relative and provisional forms previously assumed by the work of God on earth seemed by comparison unworthy of the name. Thus, while he would not have denied that the Old Testament institutions represented a real kingdom of God, the high sense with which he had invested the term made it unnatural for him to apply it to these.

And after all the Old Testament itself had pointed the way to this restricted usage followed by our Lord. Side by side with the kingdom that *is* we meet in the Old Testament a kingdom *yet to come*. This is due to three causes. In the first place, among the Semitic tribes the kingship very often originated by some powerful personality performing great acts of deliverance and obtaining in result of this a position of preeminence, as we see it happen in the case of Saul. Thus, though Jehovah was King, he nevertheless could perform acts in the future, work deliverances for his people, such as would render him King in a new sense (cf. Isa 24:21; 43:15; 52:7; Micah 2:12; 4:6; Obad 21; Ps 97:1; 99:1). Secondly, the suspension of the visibly exercised rule of Jehovah during the exile naturally led to the representation, that he would in the future become King by resuming his reign. It is especially in the Book of Daniel that the idea of the future kingdom of Jehovah is developed in contrast with the world-monarchies through which his kingdom appeared in abeyance for the present. Thirdly, the rise of Messianic prophecy had the natural result of projecting the true kingdom of God into the future. If not the present king was the ideal representative of Jehovah, but the future ruler as the prophets depict him, then, as a correlate of this, the thought would suggest itself that with this new ideal instrument the rule of God in its full ideal sense will first be realized. The expectation of the kingdom of God became equivalent to the Messianic hope of Israel. Now, inasmuch as our Lord knew himself to be the promised Messiah and knew that the Messianic King had had his typical predecessors under the Old Testament, we can indirectly show that the conception of the theocracy as a typical kingdom of God cannot have been unfamiliar to him.

In the Gospels both the thing and the name of the kingdom appear familiar to the people among whom Jesus taught (cf. Matt 3:2; Mark 15:43; Luke 14:15; 17:20). It would be rash, however, to infer from this, that Jesus simply accommodated himself in his mode of speech about the kingdom to the prevailing usage of his time. The way in which he handled the conception in general not only, but the very prominence to which he raised it, bore the marks of great originality and were productive of the most momentous changes from a religious point of view. This can be best apprehended if we place our Lord's usage by the side of that found in the contemporary Jewish literature. Here, as in the Old Testament, besides the divine kingship over the world both the present reign of Jehovah over Israel and his future kingdom are referred to. In these references we notice two peculiarities. The first is that the kingdom itself is not strictly speaking represented as future, but only the enforcement or manifestation of the kingdom. God's rule is ever existing, only at present it is not recognized. In the future the world will be made to submit to it, thus the kingdom is manifested. This peculiarity is the result of the one-sided manner in which the relation of God to his people and the world appeared to be bound up in the law. Hence the Jewish phrase, "to take up the yoke of the kingdom of heaven," meaning to vow obedience to the law. The second peculiarity consists in the rareness with which even in this qualified sense the Jewish sources speak of God's kingdom as a future thing. In comparatively few cases, where the new order of things expected in the Messianic age is referred to, does the name kingdom of God appear in connection with it. This cannot be accidental. Probably the reason is as follows: the conception which the average Jewish mind had framed of the new order of things and the interest which in its view attached to it, were not sufficiently God-centered to favor the use of the phrase "kingdom of God." The emphasis was placed largely on what the expected state would bring for Israel in a national and temporal sense. Hence it was preferably thought of as the kingdom of Israel over the other nations. Or the place of the kingdom-idea was taken by different conceptions, such as that of "the coming age," which were indefinite enough to leave room for the cherishing of the same self-centered hope.

Now it is from a comparison with these two peculiarities that our Lord's preference for the name "kingdom of God" receives its proper light. While to the mind of Judaism the divine rule is equivalent to the sovereignty of the law, Jesus, though not excluding this, knew of a much larger sphere in which God would through saving acts exercise his glorious prerogatives of kingship on a scale and in a manner unknown before. In his teaching the kingdom once more becomes a kingdom of grace as well as of law, and thus the balance so beautifully preserved in the Old Testament is restored.

The consequence of this was, of course, that great emphasis had to be thrown upon the newness of the kingdom, upon the fact of its being and bringing something more than the reign of law in which the Jews found their ideal. Thus the Lord's method of not calling even the Old Testament legal organization the kingdom may have been partly due to a revolt in his mind from the Jewish perversion of the same. Further, by making the idea as prominent as he did in his teaching and at the same time speaking of it exclusively as the kingdom of God, our Lord protested against the popular misconception of it as a national kingdom intended to bring Israel supremacy and glory. Finally, through the enlargement which the idea of God's reign had undergone, so that it stood for a reign of saving grace as well as of law, it became possible for our Lord to subsume under the notion of the kingdom the entire complex of blessing and glory which the coming order of things would involve for the people of God, and yet to keep before men's minds the thought that this new world of enjoyment was to be enjoyed as a world of God. Thus by bringing the name of "God's kingdom" and the whole content of the Messianic hopes of Israel together, he imparted to the latter the highest ideal character, a supreme religious consecration.

CHAPTER 3

KINGDOM AND KINGSHIP:

THE KINGDOM OF GOD AND THE KINGDOM OF HEAVEN

The Greek word *basileia* (βασιλεία) used in the Gospels for "kingdom" and the corresponding Hebrew and Aramaic words, such as *malkuth* (מַלְכוּת) and *mamlakhah* (מַמְלָכָה), can, like many words in the English language, designate the same conception from two distinct points of view. They may stand for the kingdom as something abstract, the *kingship or rule* exercised by the king. Or they may describe the kingdom as something concrete, the territory, the sum total of the subjects and possessions ruled over, including whatever of rights, privileges and advantages are enjoyed in this sphere. Now the question arises, in which sense did our Lord mean the phrase when he spoke of the "kingdom of God." In the Old Testament where a kingdom is ascribed either to Jehovah or to some human power, the abstract sense is usually the one intended, although in some of the latest writings of the Old Testament examples of the concrete usage occur, with reference always, however, to human kingdoms. God's kingdom is here always his reign, his rule, never his domain. When Obadiah predicts "the kingdom shall be the Lord's," his meaning is that in the future to Jehovah will belong the supremacy. That such was also the common Jewish usage in our Lord's time appears from the manner in which the supremacy of Israel over the nations is associated with the idea of the kingdom.

We have already seen that the relative absence of the phrase "the kingdom of God" from the Jewish sources points to the same conclusion, for it was a lack of interest in the truth that Jehovah would be supreme that prevented this phrase from becoming popular. On the other hand, to Jesus the thought that God would rule was a glorious thought which filled his soul with the most sacred joy. In so far it is undoubtedly correct when modern writers insist that in interpreting our Lord's sayings the meaning "reign," "kingship," shall be our point of departure, and warn against the misleading associations of the English word "kingdom," which in modern usage practically always means the territory or realm. Still it is advisable to proceed slowly here. Attention has already been called to the significant enlargement which Jesus introduced into the current use of the phrase. If to him it covered all the privileges and blessings which flow from the coming reign of God, then it is plain how inevitably it would tend in his mouth to become a concrete designation. From meaning at first "a rule" it would begin to mean, if not a territory or body of subjects, at least a realm, a sphere of life, a state of things, all of these more or less locally conceived. To be sure, even so the connotation would always remain, that the kingdom thus understood is possessed and therefore pervaded by God, but after all the rendering "reign of God" would no longer apply. In point of fact a single glance at the Gospel-discourses shows how utterly impossible it is to carry through the abstract rendering in each single instance where our Lord speaks of the kingdom of God.

Briefly stated the matter stands as follows: In a few instances the translation "reign" is required by the connection, as when it is said "the Son of man shall come in his kingdom." In some other cases, less rare than the foregoing, it is possible, perhaps slightly more plausible, to adopt the abstract rendering, as when we read of the kingdom "coming," "appearing," "being at hand," "being seen," although in these and other instances no one can maintain that the substitution of the concrete would make the sense unnatural. While neither meaning is unsuitable, one may in such cases for general reasons be inclined to believe, that the thought of a revelation of God's royal power lay uppermost in our Lord's mind. Then there are a great number, perhaps the majority, of passages in which the note of the concrete plainly predominates. When the figure is that of "calling" to the kingdom of God, of "entering" into it, of its being "shut" or of people being "cast out" from it, of its being "sought," "given," "possessed," "received," "inherited," everybody feels, that in such modes of speech not the exercise of the divine rule itself, but the resulting order of things, the complex of blessings produced by it, the sphere in which it works, stand before the speaker's mind. Taking this into consideration we may say that, if *basileia* (βασιλεία) is everywhere to be rendered by the same word, that word ought to be "kingdom." To introduce a distinction and translate in some cases "reign," in other cases "kingdom," is obviously impracticable, because, as above stated, in a number of cases we have no data for choosing between the two.

Even less satisfactory is the recent proposal to translate everywhere "the sovereignty of God," for not only is this unsuitable for all sayings in which the concrete usage of the term is undoubtedly followed, it also fails to express with fullness and accuracy the abstract sense where this may be recognized. Sovereignty denotes a relation existing by right, even where it is not actually enforced. In the case of God, therefore, it can be scarcely said to come. The divine *basileia* (βασιλεία) includes, as we have seen, besides a right to rule, the actual energetic forth-putting of God's royal power in acts of salvation.

Besides "the kingdom of God" we find "the kingdom of heaven." The Evangelist Matthew uses this well-nigh exclusively; only in 6:33; 12:28; 13:43; 21:31, 43; 26:29, does he write "the kingdom of God" or "the kingdom of my" or "their Father," whereas "the kingdom of heaven" occurs more than thirty times in his Gospel. In Matt 12:28 the use of "God" instead of "heaven" is explained by the preceding "Spirit of God"; in the two other instances in Matt 21:1, no reason for the substitution is apparent. In Mark and Luke "the kingdom of heaven" is not found. This raises the question, which of these two versions more literally reproduces the usage of Jesus himself. In all probability Matthew's does, since no good reason can be assigned, why he should have substituted "the kingdom of heaven," whilst a sufficiently plausible reason for the opposite procedure on the part of Mark and Luke can be found, in the fact, that, writing for Gentile readers, they might think such a typically Jewish phrase, as "the kingdom of heaven" less intelligible than the plain "kingdom of God." Of course, in holding this, we need not imply that in each individual case, where the first Evangelist has "kingdom of heaven," this phrase was actually employed by Jesus. All we mean to affirm is the general proposition that Jesus used both phrases, and that in so far Matthew has preserved for us an item of information no longer obtainable from the other two Synoptical Gospels.

But what were the origin and meaning of this phrase "the kingdom of heaven," and what light does it throw on our Lord's conception of the kingdom? Among the later Jews a tendency existed to forego employing the name of God. Various substitutes were current and "heaven" was one of these. Apart from the phrase under discussion, traces of this mode of speech are found in Matt 16:19; Mark 11:30; Luke 15:18, 21. It was a mode of speech which had arisen from the Jewish habit of emphasizing in the nature of God more than anything else his exaltation above the world and unapproachable majesty, to such an extent even as to endanger what must ever be the essence of religion, a true communion between God and man. But this custom, though exponential of a characteristic fault of Judaism, had also its good side, else our Lord would not have adopted it. In his human nature Jesus had a profound sense of the infinite distance between God and the creature. Whatever there was of genuine religious fear and reverence of God in the Jewish consciousness awakened an echo in his heart and found in him its ideal expression, from which all the one-sidedness that belonged to it in Judaism had disappeared. If, therefore, Jesus spoke of God as heaven, this did not spring from a superstitious fear of naming God, but rather from a desire to name him in such a way as to call up at once the most exalted conception of his being and character. To do this the word "heaven" was eminently fitted since it draws man's thought upwards to the place where God reveals his glory in perfection.

This can best be felt in another phrase which likewise among the Evangelists Matthew alone has preserved for us, and which likewise our Lord had in common with the Jewish teachers of that age, the phrase "the Father in heaven" or "the heavenly Father." If in this the name "Father" expresses the condescending love and grace of God, his infinite nearness to us, the qualification "in heaven" adds the reminder of his infinite majesty above us, by which the former ought always to be held in balance lest we injure the true spirit of religion. It may be affirmed, therefore, that, when Jesus referred to "the kingdom of heaven," he meant this in no other sense than "the kingdom of God," except in so far as there was an added note of emphasis on the exalted nature of him whose kingdom this is.

The word "heaven," however, although it primarily qualifies God and describes his greatness, not that of the kingdom, must also have been intended by our Lord to color the conception of the latter. If the king be one who concentrates in himself all the glory of heaven, what must his kingdom be? We shall not go far amiss in saying that Jesus desired to awaken in his disciples a sense of the mysterious supernatural character, of the absolute perfection and grandeur, of the supreme value pertaining to this new order of things, and desired them to view and approach it in a spirit appreciative of these holy qualities. Although the phrase "kingdom of heaven" is not found in the Old Testament, the word "heaven" appears there already in significant association with the idea of the future kingdom. In Daniel it is said that "the God of heaven" will set up a kingdom, and this means that the new reign will take its origin in a supernatural manner from the higher world. To Jesus also "heaven" and the supernatural were cognate ideas (cf. Matt 16:17; Mark 11:30). That the thought of the absolute perfection of the heavenly world as determinative of the character of the kingdom may well have been associated with the name "kingdom of heaven" in Jesus' mind, appears from the close connection between the second and third petitions in the Lord's prayer: "Thy kingdom come—Thy will be done, as in heaven, so on earth" (cf. also Matt 5:48). For heaven as the sphere of supreme unchangeable values and the goal of aspiration we may refer to such words as Matt 5:12; 6:20. In view of the profound significance which Jesus throughout ascribed to the contrast between the heavenly and the earthly world, it is hardly likely that heaven was to him a mere formal circumlocution for God. It meant not God in general, but God as known and revealed in those celestial regions which had been our Lord's eternal home. Only with this in mind can we hope to understand something of the profound sense in which he called the kingdom "a kingdom of heaven."

CHAPTER 4

THE PRESENT AND THE FUTURE KINGDOM

We have already seen that our Lord makes a sharp distinction between the Old Testament order of things and the kingdom of God, and in doing this conforms to that side of the Old Testament representation which itself looks upon the kingdom as future. Now the very important question arises: how did he conceive of the coming of this kingdom both as to time and manner? Until not long ago the view quite generally prevailed and was thought to be in harmony with Jesus' own teaching, that the coming referred to might be conceived of as a lengthy process covering ages and reaching its consummation by a sudden crisis at the end coinciding with the second coming of Christ and the end of the present world. And this prolonged process, in distinction from the final crisis, was supposed to consist in our Lord's view of essentially inward, spiritual, invisible changes. The kingdom, it was believed, comes when the gospel is spread, hearts are changed, sin and error overcome, righteousness cultivated, a living communion with God established. In this sense the kingdom began its coming when Jesus entered upon his public ministry, his work upon earth, including his death, was part of its realization, the disciples were in it, the whole subsequent history of the church is the history of its gradual extension, we ourselves can act our part in its onward movement and are members of it as a present organization.

In recent years, however, this view has been subjected to severe criticism by a certain group of writers and rejected as unhistorical. It is claimed, that Jesus took an entirely different view of the matter than that outlined above. Jesus did not for a moment think that by his prophetic activity or by any spiritual changes thus wrought among Israel, the kingdom would come. All that he meant to accomplish by his labors was merely preparatory to its coming: the people had to be made ready for its appearance. To introduce the kingdom was God's work, not his. No man could do anything towards either hastening or delaying it. And when it came it would come at one single stroke, by a sudden supernatural interposition of God, in a great world-crisis, consequently not for a part but with its whole content all at once, fulfilling all the promises, giving the signal by its arrival for the end of the present world. And this stupendous event Jesus expected to happen in his lifetime, or, after he had attained to the certainty of his intervening death, at least within the time of the then living generation.

Before endeavoring to test which of these two opposing views is in accord with our Lord's teaching, we must carefully note the real point of divergence between them and must also make clear to ourselves what issues are at stake in our decision in favor of the one or the other. The two views have this in common that they both recognize the coming of the kingdom in its final absolute sense to have been associated by Jesus with the end of the world. The older view therefore is inclusive of the more recent one, and the difference arises from the fact that the former affirms something more which the latter denies. The sole point in dispute concerns our right to ascribe to Jesus such a conception of the kingdom that he could also find the beginning of its arrival in the purely spiritual results of his labors and accordingly extend this gradual coming of it over an indefinite period of time.

But this sole point at issue is fraught with the gravest consequences as it is decided one way or the other. For, first of all, it involves the question of the infallibility of our Lord as a religious teacher. If he expected and announced only one coming of the kingdom and that to happen shortly within his lifetime or the lifetime of that generation—then there is no escape from the conclusion that the outcome has proved him mistaken. Secondly, the distribution of emphasis in our Lord's teaching becomes essentially different if we adopt the most modern view on this matter. By common consent the center of gravity in his preaching, that to which he attaches supreme importance, is the kingdom. Now, if we may believe that this kingdom was to him in part identical with the existence of certain spiritual states, such as righteousness and communion with God, then these receive with the kingdom the highest place in our Lord's estimation of values. If, on the other hand, these lie outside of the kingdom and are mere preparatory states, then they lose their central position and become means to an ulterior end consisting in the kingdom. In the third place, the controversy affects the character of our Lord's ethics. The advocates of the recent view believe that Jesus' conviction with reference to the rapidly approaching end of the world largely colored his ethical views, in that it prevented him from developing a positive interest for the duties which pertain to this present life. Finally, the conception of our Lord's character itself may be said to be involved. Some at least who ascribe to him such high-strung expectations seek to explain this on the theory, that he was an ecstatic visionary person, rather than a man of calm, equable spiritual temper. It thus appears that the aspect of our Lord's kingdom-doctrine now under discussion is interlinked with the gravest problems touching the value and authority of his character and work in general.

It must be admitted that the Old Testament does not distinguish between several stages or phases in the fulfilment of the promises regarding the kingdom, but looks upon its coming as an undivided whole. John the Baptist also seems to have still occupied this Old Testament standpoint. This, however, was due to the peculiar character of prophecy in general, in which there is a certain lack of perspective, a vision of things separated in time on one plane. We may not argue from this, that Jesus, who was more than a prophet and stood face to face with the reality, must have been subject to the same limitations. Nor are we justified in saying, that, because contemporary Judaism took such a view of the matter, Jesus likewise must have held this. For, on the one hand, Judaism was no norm for him; on the other hand, within Judaism itself a distinction between successive stages in the fulfillment of the Messianic promises had already arisen.

We have seen that the Jews were accustomed to look forward not so much to an entirely new and first arrival of the kingdom, but rather to a manifestation of God's rule in a higher form. And even within the limits of this future manifestation of the kingdom stages had begun to be distinguished. The idea of a preliminary Messianic kingdom on earth lasting for a definite number of years, to be followed by the consummation of the world and an eternal kingdom under totally new conditions may possibly have been developed as early as our Lord's day. In the later teaching of the New Testament a somewhat similar distinction certainly exists, as when Paul distinguishes between the present reign of Christ, dating from the resurrection, and the final state after he shall have delivered the kingdom to the Father (1 Cor 15:23–28).

The view, therefore, that the kingdom might be present in one sense, and yet have to come in another, did not lie beyond the doctrinal horizon of Judaism even, and we must a priori reckon with the possibility that in some form or other this view may appear also in the teaching of Jesus. In point of fact certain statements of Jesus concerning the kingdom as an inward spiritual state strongly resemble the Jewish representation, e. g. the words in Mark 10:15 about "receiving the kingdom of God" sound like an adaptation of the Jewish figure which speaks of "taking up the yoke of the kingdom of heaven" (cf. also Matt 13:52).

The difference between this Jewish representation and Jesus' idea of the preliminary kingdom lies in this, that according to the Jewish view the kingdom is always there, it being only a question whether man will take it upon himself, whereas according to Jesus, who thought less of human efforts, but had a deeper insight into the sinfulness of man and a higher conception of what the true reign of God involves, even this partial kingdom must first come through an act of God before man can be invited to receive it. As to the other point of contact in the Jewish expectation, it should be remembered that the intermediate kingdom was to begin with the appearance of the Messiah. If then Jesus regarded himself even while on earth as the Messiah and as engaged in Messianic work, which we have no reason to doubt, he must also have looked upon the stage of this earthly Messianic labor as a provisional stage of realization of the kingdom. Of course here again he transformed the Jewish conception by his spiritualizing touch into something entirely different and infinitely higher than what it was before.

Coming to the facts themselves we observe that no one denies the presence of the idea of a spiritual provisional kingdom in the gospel record of Jesus' teaching as it lies before us. The view that Jesus did not entertain this idea, of necessity involves ascribing to the Evangelists an unhistorical representation of what our Lord actually taught. It is alleged that the gospel-tradition on this point was colored by the later development of things, which showed that a long time had to intervene between the first and second coming of the Lord and therefore compelled the assuming of a provisional kingdom of protracted duration. Upon this critical phase of the question our present limits and purposes forbid us to enter. We only note it to remark that for those who hold to the historical trustworthiness of the Gospels no doubt can here exist. The present spiritual kingdom is by common consent plainly recognized in such sayings as Matt 11:11; 13:41; 16:19.

Apart, however, from critical attempts to eliminate this element from Jesus' teaching efforts have been made to attain the same object by means of exegesis, and into these we must briefly look while examining the available evidence. Clearest of all seem the words spoken by our Lord in answer to the Pharisees who had accused him of being in league with Beelzebub: "If I by the Spirit (Luke 11:20: "finger") of God cast out demons, then the kingdom of God has come upon you." The underlying supposition of this argument is, that, where the kingdom of Satan is destroyed, there of necessity the kingdom of God begins. If the former already took place at that time, then the latter also had become a present reality. Now it has been urged, that this saying proves nothing in favor of the usual conception of a spiritual kingdom to be gradually realized, because our Lord might look upon the casting out of demons and other miracles as signals of the rapidly approaching final coming of the kingdom, the beginning as it were of the end.

In answer to this we observe that, even if this were a correct interpretation, the presence of a certain element of gradualness in our Lord's conception of the matter would thereby be in principle admitted. The coming would not be entirely abrupt, there would be not only premonitions but actual anticipations. But it is impossible to interpret the words in the above sense, because at an early point of his career our Lord looked forward to his death as something that had to intervene before all things could be fulfilled, so that he could not have regarded his conquest over the demons as immediately preceding and heralding the end. His meaning must be, that when Satan's power ceases, a new order of things begins, which *in itself* is equivalent to the rule of God. In one respect only it will have to be conceded that the saying under discussion does not embody the full idea of the spiritual kingdom of God. It proves the actual presence of the kingdom at the time of our Lord's ministry, but does not directly affirm that this kingdom has its reality in inward, invisible states. The casting out of demons like other miracles belongs rather to the outward, visible sphere.

The same qualification will have to apply to another passage at least in one of the two renderings of which it is capable. According to Luke 17:21, Jesus answered the question of the Pharisees as to the time of the appearance of the kingdom of God by declaring "behold the kingdom of God is ἐντὸς ὑμῶν [*entos humōn*]." This may mean: "within you," or it may mean "in your midst." In the former case both the spiritual nature and the present reality are affirmed, in the latter case only the presence of the kingdom in some form at the time of speaking is implied. Recently it has been asserted that on the rendering "'in your midst" even the last-mentioned inference is not warranted, because our Lord speaks of the future, and means to say: at its final appearance the kingdom of God does not come so as to be subject to observation or calculation; people will not be able to say, "Here or there," lo, all at once it will be in your midst. But this is untenable because from other sayings we know, that the final coming of the kingdom is preceded by certain signs and in so far is actually subject to observation and calculation. We must choose between the two renderings given above, and of these the second, "in your midst," deserves the preference for two reasons: first, because it suits best the purpose of the question of the Pharisees, which was as to the time of the coming of the kingdom, not as to its sphere, and because of the unbelieving Pharisees it could scarcely be said that the kingdom was "*within*" them. Our Lord means to teach the enquirers that, instead of a future thing to be fixed by apocalyptic speculation, the coming of the kingdom is a present thing, present in the very midst of those who are curious about the day and the hour of its sometime appearance. Now this does not directly explain how the kingdom is present. The view remains possible that Jesus referred to miraculous works as one form of the manifestation of God's royal power, in which case this saying would not carry us beyond the foregoing about the casting out of demons. But the view is equally plausible, that he referred to the establishment of God's rule in the midst of Israel through the spiritual results of his labors.

Another statement which clearly teaches both the actual presence of the kingdom and its spiritual form of existence is

Matt 11:12; Luke 16:16 "the law and the prophets" are said to extend until John, that is to say, the prophetic looking-forward dispensation of the old covenant reaches its close in John: from there onward begins a dispensation in which the kingdom of God is the theme no longer of prophecy, but of gospel-preaching, therefore is no longer future but present. John himself is not in this kingdom while others are. This, of course, cannot apply to the final kingdom, for from this Jesus certainly could not have excluded the Baptist. It can only mean, that John does not share in the privileges made available in the new order of things introduced by Jesus' work, because he virtually continued to stand on the basis of the law and the prophets, on the basis of the old covenant. And these privileges to which John had no access certainly consisted not in the mere opportunity to witness the miracles of Jesus as external acts; a participation of inward spiritual blessings must be referred to, for on account of this our Lord pronounces the smallest or smaller in the kingdom greater than John, and we know from other sayings that Jesus measured true greatness in a different way than by contact with his miracles.

The well-known saying from the Sermon on the Mount: "Seek ye first his kingdom and his righteousness and all these things (i.e., food and raiment) shall be added unto you" (Matt 6:33), may also be quoted in this connection. Even though the view that righteousness is here present righteousness and as such a closer specification of the kingdom, should be subject to dispute, the fact remains that the kingdom itself appears as a possession obtainable in this life. For food and clothing are here represented as something to be added not to the seeking of the kingdom but to the kingdom itself, and it goes without saying, that this is applicable only to the kingdom in its present state of existence.

Most clearly, however, both the present reality and the internal nature of the kingdom are taught in some of the great parables, Matt 13; Mark 4; Luke 8. In the parable of the wheat and the tares the kingdom appears as a state of things in which the good and the bad still intermingle. The same is true of the parable of the fish-net. Here, then, obviously our Lord speaks of the kingdom in a form different from its final form, which is represented as beginning with the separation between the two kinds. Now these two parables, and the interpretation of the second, especially in Matt 13:36–43, are said to betray the influence of later conceptions. But what shall we say about the one of the mustard seed and the leaven? It cannot be denied that Jesus here conceives of the kingdom as a growing organism, a leavening power, conceptions which will scarcely apply to anything else than to a spiritual order of things. To interpret these as describing the immense contrast between the small beginning of things in Jesus' miracles and the great world-renewing conclusion of his work soon to be witnessed is, it seems to us, a forced exegesis, which unnecessarily charges Jesus with an artificial use of these figures so exquisitely chosen and so strikingly applied on the common view. Finally, it should be noted that in connection with these parables Jesus spoke significantly of "the mysteries" or "the mystery" (Mark) of the kingdom of heaven. The most plausible explanation of this statement is, that it refers not so much to the parabolic form of teaching as to the principal idea embodied in some of these parables. What else could so suitably have been designated by Jesus "a mystery" in comparison with the Jewish expectations than the truth that the kingdom comes gradually, imperceptibly, spiritually?

It appears from the foregoing that it is impossible to deny to our Lord the conception of an internal kingdom which as such comes not at once but in a lengthy process. Some writers, recognizing the necessity of this, are yet unwilling to admit that it was a conception held by Jesus from the beginning of his ministry. In their opinion his mind underwent a development on the subject; beginning with the expectation of a kingdom to appear suddenly by an immediate act of God, he afterwards became convinced that the opposition offered to his person and work rendered this impossible, that the kingdom of glory could not immediately be realized, and thus was led to believe, that only on its internal, invisible side the rule of God could even now be established. The opposition encountered would lead to his death, but death would be a transition to an exalted state, which would in turn be followed by his coming with the clouds of heaven and the establishment of the kingdom in its full final form.

A single glance at the Gospels, however, will show how impossible it is to distribute the sayings relating to the present and final form of the kingdom in such a way as to make out a period at the beginning of which Jesus knew only the latter. Some of the clearest utterances regarding the spiritual coming of the kingdom belong to a comparatively early stage of his teaching (cf. Matt 11:11; Mark 2:18–22). Nor do the general arguments adduced in favor of this hypothesis have sufficient force to commend it. It is true Jesus began with representing the kingdom as future, but this applied at the beginning equally to its spiritual, and to its visible, final realization. He urged the disciples continually to seek after the kingdom, but this only implies that within them it has to come ever increasingly. He speaks of the eschatological kingdom as "the kingdom" absolutely, but this mode of speech is not confined to the early period of his teaching: it occurs also later at a time when he is admitted to have been familiar with the idea of an immanent kingdom. He could thus speak because only at the end of time will the kingdom in its ideal completeness appear. This does not exclude that he recognized less complete embodiments of the kingdom-idea as present long before. Again it is true that he does not at first announce himself as Messiah, and from this the inference might be drawn that with his Messiahship he put also the coming of the kingdom into the future. This inference would be correct, if restraint in the announcement of himself as Messiah had proceeded from the conviction that he was not as yet the Messiah, nor his present work Messianic work in the strict sense of the term. In point of fact Jesus kept his Messianic claims in the background for pedagogical reasons, while perfectly conscious that he was exercising Messianic functions. The correct view on this point is that he distinguished two forms of Messianic activity, one on earth in humility, one from the throne of glory, and corresponding to this two forms of the kingdom, one invisible now, one visible at the end, and, thus understood, the two-sidedness of his Messianic consciousness affords a striking parallel to the two-sidedness of his kingdom-conception. On the whole, therefore, we have no reason to believe that in our Lord's subjective apprehension of the truth there was any appreciable progress on this important subject within the limits of his public ministry.

In Jesus' objective teaching, on the other hand, as distinguished from his subjective consciousness, a certain development in the presentation of truth concerning the kingdom cannot be denied. We are able to affirm this, not so much from a comparison of the utterances belonging to the earlier or later periods. This would be difficult since the material in our Gospels is not all arranged on the chronological plan. The fact appears rather in this way, that at two points in our Lord's ministry a certain phase of the doctrine of the kingdom is introduced with such emphasis as to mark it relatively new. These two points are the occasion on which our Lord uttered the great kingdom-parables and the announcement of his passion near Caesarea Philippi.

From the manner in which the great parables draw the distinction between the immanent and eschatological coming of the kingdom, and from the elaborateness with which Jesus here describes the gradual, invisible character of the former as resembling the process of organic growth, we are led to infer that previously this principle had not been accentuated in his teaching. This does not mean that he had hitherto abstained from referring to the spiritual side of the subject. We have seen above that the opposite is true. It simply means, that up to this point, while sometimes predicating of the kingdom things true of it in its purely spiritual stage, sometimes predicating of it things of eschatological character, he did not on purpose formulate the difference and the relation between the two, but treated the kingdom as a unit of which both classes of statements could be equally affirmed. The historical explanation of this peculiarity is probably to be sought in our Lord's desire to keep in close touch during the first period of his ministry with the Old Testament type of teaching, which, as we have seen, did not as yet distinguish between periods and stages in the realization of the kingdom. Thus in condescension to Israel he took up the thread of revelation where the Old Testament had left it, to give a new and richer development to it soon after in his epoch-making parabolic deliverances. The new element introduced at the second critical juncture, in the region of Caesarea Philippi, concerns the relation of the church to the kingdom and will be discussed afterwards in a separate chapter.

It should be observed that our Lord's teaching relates to two aspects of the same kingdom, not to two separate kingdoms. The ancient theological distinction between a kingdom of grace and a kingdom of glory is infelicitous for this reason. In the parable the growing of the grain and the harvest belong together as connected parts of the same process. There is one continuous kingdom-forming movement which first lays hold upon the inward spiritual center of life by itself, and then once more seizes the same in connection with its external visible embodiment. In the second stage the essence of the first is re-included and remains of supreme importance. The immanent kingdom as at first realized continues to partake of imperfections. Hence the eschatological crisis will not merely supply this soul of the kingdom with its fitting body, but will also bring the ideal perfection of the inner spirit itself. Our Lord's doctrine of the two-sided kingdom thus understood is an eloquent witness to the unique energy with which he subordinated the physical to the spiritual, as well as to the sobriety with which he upheld the principle, that the physical is not to be despised, but appreciated in its regenerated form, as the natural and necessary instrument of revelation for the spiritual.

CHAPTER 5

CURRENT MISCONCEPTIONS REGARDING
THE PRESENT AND FUTURE KINGDOMS

Having found that both the immanent and the eschatological conceptions of the coming of the kingdom are clearly represented in Jesus' teaching and having in general defined the relation of the one to the other, we may now proceed to look at each separately in order to guard against certain misconceptions to which both may easily become subject. A tendency exists with some writers, especially of the class who insist that Jesus had no other than the eschatological conception of the kingdom, to identify the view ascribed to him with the current Jewish expectations. This would involve, that he was not only mistaken in regard to the time of the kingdom's appearance, but also held an inherently false idea regarding its nature, not having entirely outgrown the limitations of his age and environment on this point. It has in all seriousness been asserted by a recent writer of this class, that the notion of the kingdom in the historic form in which our Lord embraced it, is that element of his teaching to which we cannot ascribe abiding value, that in the experience of Jesus himself it proved a delusion, that to his teaching on the fatherhood of God rather than to it is due the enrichment which our Lord wrought in the religious consciousness of humanity.

This error results from the failure to recognize the immanent, spiritual aspect of the kingdom-idea as actually present in Jesus' teaching and the thorough re-construction which in result of it the idea as a whole underwent. It was little more than the name that Jesus borrowed from the kingdom-expectation of Judaism; whatever of the content of his own kingdom-teaching he had in common with the eschatological belief of his time belonged to the purer and nobler type of Jewish eschatology, that built up around the idea of "the coming age." And even the latter he lifted to an infinitely higher plane by subsuming it under the principle of the supremacy of God. So far as connected with the kingdom the Jewish hope was intensely political and national, considerably tainted also by sensuality. From all political bearings our Lord's teaching on the kingdom was wholly dissociated (cf. Mark 12:13; John 18:36). There is no trace in the Gospels of the so-called chiliastic expectation of a provisional political kingdom, that strange compromise whereby Judaism endeavored to reconcile the two heterogeneous elements that struggled for the supremacy in its eschatological consciousness. What formally corresponds in our Lord's teaching to this notion is the idea of the invisible, spiritual kingdom, and how totally different it is!

Equally broad and free is Jesus' kingdom-doctrine in its attitude towards the problem of Israel's national prerogative.

Sayings like Matt 8:11; 21:43; 28:19; Mark 13:10; 14:9; Luke 4:26–27, prove that he distinctly anticipated the rejection of many in Israel and the extension of the gospel to the Gentiles on a large scale. It is true these are all prophetic words. In his own pastoral activity he confined himself deliberately to the lost sheep of the house of Israel and kept his helpers within the same limits. But even so there is in his whole attitude as a teacher of Israel that which has been strikingly characterized as "intensive universalism." In the Jew it is the man he seeks and endeavors to save. The problems raised, the duties required, the blessings conferred are such as to be applicable to all without distinction of race, caste, or sex.

Luke 22:30 is sometimes quoted to prove that Jesus had not freed himself from the Jewish particularism. Though possibly the "judging" may have to be understood in the sense of "reigning," yet the words by no means imply the salvation of all Israel, nor do they exclude the calling of the Gentiles. They were spoken at a time when Jesus could no longer doubt that the masses of Israel would reject him. Besides the words are figurative, to judge from the context with its reference to "eating" and "drinking." All we can legitimately infer from them is that the apostles will have a position of preeminence in the kingdom.

The third feature in which our Lord's kingdom-message differs from the Jewish expectation consists in the absence of the sensualistic element so prominent in the latter. True he speaks in connection with the kingdom of eating, drinking, reclining at table, inheriting the earth, etc., and it is said we have no right to spiritualize all this. But the Old Testament already used such forms of speech with the clear consciousness of their metaphorical character. Even in the apocalyptic literature this sense is not entirely wanting, as the statement of 1 Enoch 15:11,

"They will not partake of any food, nor will they thirst," shows. With reference to one point at least, Jesus positively affirmed that the sensual enjoyments of the present life will cease in the world to come (Mark 12:25). On the other hand, we must remember that it is possible to go too far in the spiritualizing interpretation of this class of utterances. We may not dissolve everything into purely inward processes and mental states, as modern theologians do when they say that heaven and hell are in the hearts of men. The eschatological kingdom has certainly in our Lord's conception its own outward forms of life. These figures stand for objective, external realities in which the body will have its own part and function. When our Lord speaks of earthly enjoyments, he means something that will be truly analogous to these and yet move on an altogether higher plane. Our difficulty lies in this, that we cannot frame a concrete conception of outward forms of life without having recourse to the senses. But our difficulty does not prove the impossibility, nor does it prove that the same difficulty existed for Jesus, who was familiar with the heavenly world by experience.

We believe, however, that there is greater need at the present day to guard against a misunderstanding of the other side of our Lord's kingdom-teaching, that which relates to the spiritual, invisible form of the kingdom. Modern writers do not always sufficiently emphasize that, notwithstanding its internal character, the kingdom remains to all intents a supernatural kingdom. It is easy to speak disparagingly of the gross realistic expectations of the Jews, but those who do so often attack under the pretense of a refined spiritualism the very essence of Biblical supernaturalism. After all deductions are made, it must be maintained that the Jews could not have cherished this vigorous realism, had they not been supernaturalists at heart, trained in that great school of supernaturalism, the, Old

Testament. In this matter Jesus was in full agreement with their position.

The circumstance that some of the parables which deal with this aspect of the kingdom have been taken from the sphere of organic life has sometimes led to misconceptions here. The point of comparison in these parables is not the naturalness of the process but only its gradualness and invisible character. In the parable of the imperceptibly growing seed (Mark 4:26–29), rather the opposite is implied, viz., that God gives the increase without human intervention. Jesus performs all his work, even that pertaining to the immanent kingdom, in the Spirit, and the Spirit stands for the supernatural. That we must not identify the processes whereby this side of the kingdom is realized with purely natural processes can be best seen from the Fourth Gospel. Here the present life is equivalent to the immanent kingdom. But this present life appears to be thoroughly supernatural in its origin and character. Regeneration introduces into it.

At a subsequent point of our enquiry, when discussing the relation of the church to the kingdom, it will appear still more clearly, that by its translation into the sphere of the internal and invisible the kingdom-idea has lost nothing of the supernaturalistic associations which belonged to it from its very origin. The difference between the two stages of its coming does not lie in that the one is brought about by forces already present in the human world, whereas the other has to be accomplished by the introduction of new miraculous forces from above. It is a difference merely in the mode of operation and revelation of the supernatural common to both stages. The same omnipotent power at work through the ages will also effect the consummation at the end. But it will assume a new form when the end has come, so as to work instantaneously, and will draw within the sphere of its operation the entire physical universe. It would not be in harmony with Jesus' view so to conceive of it, as if by the gradual extension of the divine power operating internally, by the growth of the church, by the ever-widening influence of the truth, the kingdom which now is will become all-comprehensive and universal and so of itself pass over into the final kingdom. This would eliminate all true eschatology and obliterate the distinction between the two aspects of Jesus' teaching on the subject.

The parables of the wheat and the tares and of the fish-net, while on the one hand they do imply, as we have seen, the higher unity of the entire movement, also imply on the other hand that its consummation does not spontaneously result from the preceding process, supernatural though this be. The harvest is conditioned by the ripeness of the grain, and yet the ripeness of the grain can never of itself set in operation the harvest. The harvest comes when the man puts forth the sickle, because the fruit is ripe. So when the immanent kingdom has run its course to maturity, God will intervene in the miracle of all miracles. It would also plainly be impossible for the final kingdom to come in any other way than this. For this final state of the kingdom presupposes great physical, cosmic changes, which no force working in the spiritual sphere can produce. It would be difficult to overestimate the vividness with which our Lord realized and the emphasis with which he describes the new and marvelous conditions under which the life of the blessed in the future kingdom will be lived. It is an order of things lying altogether above this earthly life, in which the righteous shall shine as the sun, in which all the prophets will be seen, in which the pure in heart shall enjoy the beatific vision of God, in which those who hunger and thirst after righteousness shall be completely filled. Surely to effect this there must take place a great crisis, a great catastrophe at the end which will be the very opposite of all evolution. Our Lord himself has marked its unique character by calling it the palingenesis, the regeneration (Matt 19:28).

Still further we must guard against confining the internal, spiritual kingdom to the sphere of the ethical. This is an error which has had considerable vogue in recent times, owing to the fact that certain systems of theology constructed from a one-sided ethical point of view have adopted the kingdom-idea as their organizing center. The kingdom has been defined as an ethical community realized by the interaction of men on the principle of love. This is erroneous in two respects. In the first place, according to our Lord the whole content of religion is to be subsumed under the kingdom. While it is true that the kingdom consists in righteousness, it is by no means coextensive with the same, but consists in many other things besides. Such blessings as life, forgiveness of sin, communion with God, belong to it just as much and have just as vital a connection with the kingdom-idea, as the cultivation of love, as will subsequently appear. And secondly, all that belongs to the kingdom, the ethical and religious alike, is represented in Jesus' kingdom-teaching, not as the product of human activity, but as the work of God. He nowhere says that men make the kingdom. In our Lord's Prayer the words: "Thy will be done" explain the preceding words "Thy Kingdom come," but both are petitions, in uttering which we are taught to look to God that he may set up in us his reign even in that form which will be revealed through our actions.

CHAPTER 6

THE ESSENCE OF THE KINGDOM:

THE KINGDOM AS THE SUPREMACY OF GOD
IN THE SPHERE OF SAVING POWER

It has been shown in the foregoing how our Lord designates the new order of things he came to introduce "the kingdom of God," and that not merely in its final outcome but in its entire course of development. The question must next be raised. Why did he adopt this name, what is the appropriateness of the designation to his own mind? It certainly would be wrong to assume that he used it from mere accommodation to a popular parlance, that it was in no wise suggestive to him of important principles and ideas. This is excluded by the fact pointed out above, that it was not by any means the most familiar of the names current among the Jews for the Messianic age. If Jesus nevertheless favored it above all others, he must have had a positive reason for this. Nor can we explain his choice from mere dependence on the Old Testament. Jesus' dependence on the Old Testament was never a mere matter of form. He always sought in the form the substance, in the terms appropriated the great ideal principles they were intended to express. We must therefore look for these. In looking for them we must not expect to find anywhere in his teaching a definition of the kingdom. Jesus' method of teaching was not the philosophical one of defining a thing, but the popular, parabolic one of describing and illustrating it. Paul, though speaking much less of the kingdom, has come much nearer to defining it than our Lord (cf. Rom 14:17). The absence of definition, however, does not involve a lack of order or correlation in the aspects and features described. In the great variety of statements made concerning the kingdom the careful observer will not fail to discover certain general lines along which the description or comparison moves, certain outstanding principles to whose elucidation it constantly returns. If we can ascertain these, we shall also have found the key to our Lord's own view about the deeper meaning of the name "kingdom of God."

At the outset we must reject as inadequate the favorite modern explanation that in the figure of the kingdom the point of comparison lies primarily in the mutual association of men so as to form a moral or religious organism. The kingdom is indeed a community in which men are knit together by the closest of bonds, and especially in connection with our Lord's teaching on the church this is brought out. Taking, however, the kingdom-teaching as a whole this point is but little emphasized, Matt 13:24–30, 47–50. Besides, this conception is not nearly wide enough to cover all the things predicated of the kingdom in the Gospels, according to which it appears to consist as much in gifts and powers from above as in inter-human relations and activities. Its resemblance to a community offers at least only a partial explanation of its kingdom-character, and so far as this explanation is correct it is not ultimate, because not the union of men as such, but that in God which produces and underlies it, is the true kingdom-forming principle.

The main reason for the use of the name by Jesus lies undoubtedly in this, that in the new order of things God is in some such sense the supreme and controlling factor as the ruler in a human kingdom. The conception is a God-centered conception to the very core. In order to appreciate its significance, we must endeavor to do what Jesus did, look at the whole of the world and of life from the point of view of their subserviency to the glory of God. The difficulty for us in achieving this lies not merely in that we are apt to take a lower man-centered view of religion, but equally much in that by our modern idea of the state we are not naturally led to associate such an order of things with the name of a kingdom. According to our modern conception, especially in its republican form, the institution of the state with its magistrate exists for the sake of the subjects, even the king, at least in a constitutional monarchy, may be considered as a means to an end. In the ancient state this is different. Here the individual exists for the state, and in the Oriental monarchy the state is centralized and summed up in the person of the ruler.

Now whatever may be the merits or demerits of such a principle as the constructive principle for our human political life, it affords obviously the only point of view from which we can properly construe the fundamental relation between God and man. It was on the basis of such a conception of kingship, that from early times the relation of God to Israel had been expressed in the form of a royal rule. The primary purpose of

Israel's theocratic constitution was not to teach the world the principles of civil government, though undoubtedly in this respect also valuable lessons can be learned from it, but to reflect the eternal laws of religious intercourse between God and man as they will exist in the consummate life at the end. Judaism had lost the sense for this, had shifted the center of gravity from God to man; in Jesus' teaching the proper relation was restored. To him the kingdom exists there, where not merely God is supreme, for that is true at all times and under all circumstances, but where God supernaturally carries through his supremacy against all opposing powers and brings man to the willing recognition of the same. It is a state of things in which everything converges and tends towards God as the highest good.

The closing words of the Lord's Prayer, according to the version in Matthew, are the purest expression of this kingdom-consciousness which Jesus desired to cultivate in the minds of his disciples: "Thine is the kingdom, and the power, and the glory, forever." Even if these words should not be authentic, since they are wanting in the text of Luke, and in the text of Matthew in some important authorities, whence the Revised Version places them in the margin, still they retain their weight as a very ancient witness to the conception of the kingdom in the early church. It will be observed that Paul in 1 Cor 15, where he speaks of the delivering up of the kingdom by Christ to the Father, describes the content of the final kingdom of God in precisely the same way as consisting in this that "God will be all in all" (1 Cor 15:28; cf. Rev 11:15). Because the kingdom is thus centered in God himself, it can be represented by our Lord as the supreme object of human pursuit. This would plainly be impossible if the idea of the kingdom was conceived on any lower plane, for in that case some other object would be interposed between God and man as the absolute end of man's religious aspiration. Because the kingdom of God means the ideal of religion in this highest sense realized, Jesus declared the scribe to be not far from the kingdom, because the latter recognized the commandment to love God with all the heart, all the soul, all the strength, and all the mind as the supreme commandment (Mark 14:34). In Matt 6:33, the seeking after the kingdom is opposed to the seeking after earthly things, because it is at the bottom the seeking after God himself. And the same God-centered view, which thus finds expression in the thought of the kingdom, is also the highest aspect under which Jesus views his entire work in the discourses of the Fourth Gospel. Here Christ at the close of his ministry speaks to the Father: "I glorified thee on the earth, having accomplished the work which thou hast given me to do" (John 17:4). We find, therefore, that though the name kingdom is absent, the main idea embodied in it is found in John as well as in the Synoptists. The principle thus disclosed is of the greatest conceivable practical significance. It teaches that in the very order of things provided for the salvation of mankind, everything is in its ultimate analysis designed to glorify God. The kingdom is a conception which must of necessity remain unintelligible and unacceptable to every view of the world and of religion which magnifies man at the expense of God.

The supremacy of God in the kingdom reveals itself in various ways. It comes to light in the acts by which the kingdom is established, in the moral order under which it exists, in the spiritual blessings, privileges and delights that are enjoyed in it. The first constitute the kingdom a sphere of divine power, the second a sphere of divine righteousness, the third a sphere of divinely bestowed blessedness. These rubrics are not, of course, so many sections into which the content of the kingdom can be divided, but rather so many aspects under which it may be considered. What is kingdom-power from one point of view is kingdom-righteousness from another and kingdom-blessedness from still a third. The exercise of power is needed to render possible the realization of righteousness, the realization of righteousness to render possible the bestowal of blessedness. Remembering the descriptive character and the practical purpose of our Lord's teaching we should not endeavor to draw any hard and fast lines, but make allowance for the easy passing over of one aspect into the other.

The element of power is one of the earliest and most constant elements in the Biblical disclosure of the divine kingship. The Song of Moses celebrates Jehovah as King because he has gloriously overcome his enemies (Exod 15). And from these ancient times onward the note of conquest is never absent from the Old Testament utterances regarding the kingdom. Especially in Daniel the kingdom is presented from this side, when it appears as a stone breaking to pieces the image of the world-kingdoms (Dan 2:45). How familiar this idea was to the Apostle Paul we may gather from his words in 1 Cor 15:25, "For he (Christ) must reign, till he (God) hath put all his enemies under his feet." Here the kingship of Christ is equivalent to the process of subjecting one enemy after another. After the last enemy, death, has been conquered, there is no further need for the kingdom of Christ: hence it is delivered up to God the Father. Christ's kingdom as a process of conquest precedes the final kingdom of God as a settled permanent state.

To the Jewish conception of the coming kingdom also this feature was essential. What our Lord did was to give to this Jewish mode of representation an infinitely higher content, while formally retaining it. He lifted it out of the political sphere into the spiritual. The conquests to which he refers are those over Satan and the demons, over sin and evil. It is kingdom against kingdom, but both of these opposing kingdoms belong to a higher world than that to which Rome and her empire belong. In the words, "If I by the Spirit of God cast out demons, then the kingdom of God has come upon you" (Matt 12:28), already commented upon in another connection, our Lord refers to the forth-putting of this divine conquering power as a sure sign of the coming of the kingdom.

But we must broaden this idea: not merely the casting out of demons, all the miracles of Jesus find their interpretation at least in part from this, that they are manifestations of the kingdom-power. It is a mistake to think that Jesus looked upon them exclusively as signs authenticating his mission. Undoubtedly this was one of the purposes for which the miracles were intended, and it is brought out prominently in the Fourth Gospel. But in the Synoptists, where the teaching of Jesus is centered in the kingdom-idea, the miracles do not appear primarily in this light. Here they are signs in a different sense, viz., signs of the actual arrival of the kingdom, because they show that the royal power of God is already in motion. He rebukes the people because they can interpret the signs of the weather, but cannot interpret the signs of the times. These signs of the times are nothing else than the miraculous works which prove the kingdom to be there. The forces which will revolutionize heaven and earth are already at work.

On the same principle Jesus answered the inquiry of John the Baptist, as to whether he were the one that was to come, or they should expect another, with a reference to his Messianic works: "The blind receive their sight, and the lame walk, the lepers are cleansed, and the deaf hear, and the dead are raised up, and the poor have good tidings preached unto them" (Matt

11:5). The Messianic works are the works which inaugurate the kingdom. Still more clearly this appears from the discourse in the synagogue at Nazareth recorded by Luke, which had for its text the prophecy of Isaiah: "The Spirit of the Lord is upon me, because he anointed me to preach good tidings to the poor: he hath sent me to proclaim release to the captives, and recovering of sight to the blind, to set at liberty them that are bruised, to proclaim the acceptable year of the Lord" (Luke 4:18–19). Here the acceptable year of Jehovah, the year of jubilee, in which all things return to their normal, wholesome condition, is none other than the era of the kingdom, and by the bestowal of the blessings enumerated it comes.

It will be observed that the miracles which Jesus wrought were with one exception beneficent miracles. To give a sign from heaven, a sign not possessing this beneficent character, he persistently refused. The true signs had to be kingdom-signs, exhibitions of God's royal power. This power, therefore, has two sides: so far as the enemies of God are concerned, it is a conquering, destructive, judging power; so far as man is concerned, it is a liberating, healing, saving power. In the casting out of demons both sides are revealed. In the other miracles it is chiefly the beneficent side which finds expression. Jesus brings release to the captives and sets at liberty those that are bruised, for the satanic power not only renders man miserable but also reduces him to bondage, as is even externally indicated by the fact that the demons control the physical organism of those possessed.

The question naturally arises, how can this identification of the kingdom with the effects of a power working largely in the physical sphere be reconciled with the emphasis placed by Jesus upon the spiritual nature of the kingdom. The answer is that the physical evils which the kingdom-power removes have a moral and spiritual background. Satan reigns not merely in the body, nor merely in the mind pathologically considered, but also in the heart and will of man as the instigator of sin and the source of moral evil. Hence Jesus made his miracles the occasion for suggesting and working the profounder change by which the bonds of sin were loosed and the rule of God set up anew in the entire inner life of men. Because this real connection exists, the physical process can become symbolical of the spiritual. In the Synoptical Gospels, it is true, this is nowhere directly stated, although the external and the internal are sometimes significantly placed side by side as coordinated parts of one identical work (Mark 2:9). In the Fourth Gospel, however, Jesus gives clearly to understand that the physical acts are intended to point to corresponding spiritual acts. The healing of the blind, the raising of the dead find their counterpart in what he does for the souls of sinners.

On the other hand, it should not be overlooked that these physical signs have also a connection with the kingdom in the external sphere itself. The miraculous power is prophetic of that great kingdom-power which will be exerted at the end. It is especially in eschatological connections that a revelation of power is referred to (Matt 24:30; Mark 12:24). All the supernatural phenomena that accompanied not merely the ministry of Jesus, but characterized also the history of the apostolic church, must be interpreted in this light. It had to be shown immediately, that the work inaugurated by Jesus arrives at nothing less than a supernatural renewal of the world, whereby all evil will be overcome, a renewal of the physical as well of the spiritual world (Matt 19:28). Because the Old Testament had treated these two as belonging inseparably together, and because in reality it would now appear that the two lay far apart in point of time, it was all the more necessary that some solid anticipations of the eschatological change should be given. Verbal prophecy was not sufficient: a prophecy in acts was required, and this the miracles furnished. In so far there is an element of truth in the modern view which represents Jesus as looking upon the miracles as the beginning of the final arrival of the kingdom. Here, as on other points, our Lord's teaching warns us against that excessive spiritualizing tendency, to which the external world becomes altogether worthless and indifferent or even withdrawn from the direct control of God.

The source of this kingdom-power is, according to our Lord's teaching, the Spirit. In the saying of Matt 12:28 the point evidently is, that where the Spirit of God operates, there the kingdom of God comes. To his being anointed with the Spirit Jesus ascribes all his power to do miracles (Luke 4:18). To accuse him of casting out demons in league with Beelzebub is to blaspheme the Spirit (cf. for the interchangeableness of the conceptions of "Spirit" and "power," such passages as Luke 1:17, 35; 24:19, 49; Acts 1:8; 10:38). Indeed our Lord's references to the Spirit as the author of saving acts are almost entirely connected with his miracles. Still it would be inaccurate, as is sometimes done, to deny to Jesus the idea, so beautifully worked out by Paul, that the Spirit is the source of the moral and religious renewal of man, the author and bearer of the entire Christian life with all its graces and virtues. In the Fourth Gospel the presence of this idea is acknowledged by all. Here our Lord teaches that man must be born of water and the Spirit in order to see and to enter the kingdom of God. In the closing discourses of this Gospel the work of the Spirit as guiding all the disciples into the knowledge of the truth is made very prominent, and the knowledge of the truth in our Lord's Johannine teaching distinctly includes its moral and spiritual saving apprehension and appropriation by the disciples, so that the Spirit is here brought into direct connection with the ethical and religious life of man.

Even from the Synoptical sayings the same idea is not entirely absent. Though the Spirit may work in the sphere of the miracles, yet these miracles are wrought for the moral purpose of overthrowing the kingdom of evil. The Spirit leads Jesus into the wilderness to be tempted of Satan and thus appears as pursuing the end of the Messiah's moral victory over the Prince of Evil. Satan exerts an evil influence over man in the moral and religious sphere, consequently on the principle of opposition the Spirit of God must have been believed to exert a good influence. Probably also the saying of Jesus, that the heavenly Father out of his goodness is ready to give the Spirit to his children (Luke 11:13), does not have exclusive reference to the Spirit as the source of miracles. Thus we see that the first outlines of the doctrine of the Spirit, as afterwards developed in apostolic revelation, are already drawn by Jesus. The full disclosure of this doctrine could not be expected then, because the full bestowal of the Spirit could not come until after the Saviour's death (John 7:39). But in his Messianic works Jesus exhibited in a revelation of facts the fundamental part taken by the Spirit in the salvation of man. Thus Jesus stands at the transition point between the Old Testament doctrine of the Spirit on the one side and the full apostolic unfolding of the doctrine on the other side. In the Old Testament the emphasis still rests on the charismatic character of the Spirit's work as qualifying the office-bearers of the theocracy for their task. Jesus began to show how the official Spirit, which belongs to him as Messiah, becomes a source of communication of the Spirit to others, and that not merely for the performance of supernatural works but also for conferring the religious and moral blessings of the kingdom. The part, however, of our Lord's teaching in which the connection between the Spirit and the internal aspect of the kingdom finds clearest expression, and which approaches most closely to the apostolic type of doctrine, is that relating to the church. With this we shall deal in a later chapter.

CHAPTER 7

THE ESSENCE OF THE KINGDOM CONTINUED:

THE KINGDOM IN THE SPHERE OF RIGHTEOUSNESS

In regard to the relation between the kingdom and righteousness three lines of thought can be distinguished in the teaching of Jesus. According to the one the ideal fulfilment of the will of God in man's moral life is in itself a revelation of the divine supremacy, and the act of declaring man righteous in itself a prerogative of the divine kingship. According to the other the righteousness needed by man appears as one of the blessings which God in his kingdom bestows. According to still a third representation the kingdom is given as a reward for the practice of righteousness in this life. Each of these we shall consider separately.

According to the Old Testament and the Semitic conception generally, the kingship and the exercise of legislative and judicial authority are inseparably united. The modern distribution of these several functions of government over distinct institutions is entirely unknown. The king gives laws and executes laws. "To judge" and "to reign" are synonymous expressions. This should be kept in mind in order to apprehend correctly the first aspect of our Lord's teaching on righteousness as related to the kingdom. Righteousness is always taken by Jesus in a specific sense which it obtains from the reference to God as Lawgiver and Judge. Our modern usage of the word is often a looser one, since we are apt to associate with it no further thought than that of what is fair and equitable, inherently just. To Jesus righteousness meant all this and much more than this. It meant such moral conduct and such a moral state as are right when measured by the supreme norm of the nature and will of God, so that they form a reproduction of the latter, a revelation, as it were, of the moral glory of God.

When the disciples are exhorted to let their light shine before men that these may see their good works and glorify the Father in heaven, this thought is expressed in terms of fatherhood, but the conception of glory involved is closely allied to that of kingship. In the Lord's Prayer the petition "Thy kingdom come" naturally leads on to the petition "Thy will be done, as in heaven, so on earth," so that the fulfilment of the will of God is obviously regarded as one of the principal forms in which his kingship is realized. Its consummate expression this principle finds in the commandment: "Ye therefore shall be perfect, as your heavenly Father is perfect" (Matt 5:48). The sayings just quoted affirm not merely that the norm of righteousness is to be found in God, they likewise imply that the aim of righteousness, the final cause of obedience, lies in God.

Righteousness is to be sought from the pure desire of satisfying him, who is the supreme end of all moral existence.

In both these points our Lord's teaching on righteousness was no less vitally connected with his conception of the divine kingship than with that of the divine fatherhood. And in both respects we must place his teaching over against the principles and tendencies which were at work in the Jewish ethics of the time, in order fully to appreciate its profound significance. The characteristic faults of the Jewish ethics were formalism, casuistry, an inclination to emphasize the prohibition rather than the commandment, and, worst of all, self-righteousness and hypocrisy. These faults proceeded from a twofold source. On the one hand, Judaism had virtually become a worship of the law as such. The dead letter of the law had taken the place of the living God. The majesty and authority of the holy nature and perfect will of God were no longer felt in the commandments. On the other hand, the Jewish law-observance was self-centered, because it was chiefly intended to be the instrument for securing the blessedness of the coming age.

Where the norm of righteousness is a deified law rather than a personal lawgiver, and where the supreme motive for obedience is a self-interested one, there inevitably the faults above enumerated must make their appearance. God being kept at a distance, no strong need will be felt for yielding more than compliance with the law in the outward act. Because the ultimate root in which all the commandments are one in the nature and will of God is lost sight of, the law will become a mere aggregate of unrelated precepts, a collection of statutory ordinances, for adjusting which to the compass of the entire outward life a complicated system of the most refined casuistry will be required. Because the controlling motive is self-centered, the escape from transgression will form a more serious concern than the positive fulfilment of what the spirit of the law demands. Finally, where the moral life is thus concentrated on the outward conduct, where the conscience does not search and judge itself in the presence of the personal God, who knows the heart, there the sins of self-righteousness and hypocrisy find a fertile soil for development.

Such was the moral consciousness in which our Lord wrought a revolution by enunciating the twofold principle above stated. He once more made the voice of the law the voice of the living God, who is present in every commandment, so absolute in his demands, so personally interested in man's conduct, so all-observant, that the thought of yielding to him less than the whole inner life, the heart, the soul, the mind, the strength, can no longer be tolerated. Thus quickened by the spirit of God's personality, the law becomes in our Lord's hands a living organism, in which soul and body, spirit and letter, the greater and smaller commandments are to be distinguished, and which admits of being reduced to great comprehensive principles in whose light the weight and purport of all single precepts are to be intelligently appreciated.

The two great commandments are to love God supremely and one's neighbor as one's self (Mark 12:30–31). The practical test of conduct is to do unto men all things whatsoever one desires to have done to one's self, for this is the summary of the law and the prophets (Matt 7:12). In case of conflict the mere ceremonial must give way before the ethical (Matt 5:23–24). There are commandments in reference to which it is sufficient to say that they should not be left undone, such as the tithing of mint, anise and cumin, and there are commandments of such supreme and intrinsic importance as to demand in men a positive and energetic determination to do them, viz., the weightier matters of the law, justice, mercy and faith (Matt

23:23). Because righteousness is a matter of immediate, personal concern between the soul and God, it can rest on nothing else than the divinely revealed commandments, and no human tradition can bind the conscience: "Every plant which the heavenly Father planted not, shall be rooted up" (Matt 15:13). Finally, what alone can impart value in the sight of God to any act of obedience is the sincerity of the heart from which it proceeds. Righteousness must be fruit, the organic product of the life and character, exponential of what is within (Matt 7:16, 20; 21:43).

All this was the result of bringing men face to face with God as the righteous Lawgiver and King, personally cognizant of every man's conduct. In view of it, it is hardly necessary to observe that our Lord also represents God as the supreme Judge of the moral life. To be righteous is strictly speaking equivalent to being justified of God. And this reference to the judgment of God is to Jesus not a subordinate matter, it is an essential ingredient of his conception of righteousness. The process of moral action does not appear complete to him until it receives in the divine justifying sentence its crown and consummation. The right to hold accountable and judge ranked clearly in his mind among the highest of God's royal prerogatives. On this point he carefully preserved the valuable kernel of truth contained in the exaggerated Jewish ideas about the forensic relation between God and man. While making much of the divine love, our Lord did not suffer his emphasis on this to obscure the important principle of the divine justice. In correcting the one-sidedness of Judaism, which had no eye for the grace of God, he did not fall into the opposite extreme of reducing everything to the love of God. On the contrary, in his teaching the two divine attributes of love and justice are perfectly balanced. In the well-known saying of Matt 6:33 we can observe the close connection he assumed between the kingship of God and his forensic righteousness. The disciples are here urged, first to make God's kingdom the object of their pursuit, and then, as a closer specification, to seek God's righteousness. By the latter is meant either the exercise of God's justifying righteousness on man's behalf, or that righteousness as a human state, which is counted before God. On either view, the kingship of God and the exercise of forensic righteousness are intimately associated.

The supreme importance which Jesus in virtue of this God-centered conception attached to righteousness may be inferred from the fact that its pursuit is spoken of in equally absolute terms as the seeking of the kingdom. It is the highest concern of the disciple. He must hunger and thirst after it, treat it as the very sustenance of his life, the only thing that will satisfy his most instinctive desires. He must submit to persecution for its sake. Matt 5:6, 10. All this becomes intelligible only on the assumption that to Jesus the question of right and wrong was not a purely moral, but in the deepest sense a religious question. His teaching on righteousness means the subsumption of ethics under religion.

We need not wonder that with such a sublime conception of what righteousness implied, even this aspect of the kingdom, in which formally at least, it closely resembled the Jewish idea of the already existing reign of God through the law, appeared nevertheless to Jesus as something future. The kingdom had yet to come, because it consisted in an observance of the law conformed to an altogether new ideal, practiced in an altogether new spirit. Something far greater and higher stood before his mind than had ever been contemplated by the mind of Judaism. Thus the God-centered ideal of righteousness itself prepared the way for the second line of thought traceable in our

Lord's teaching on the subject, viz., that righteousness is one of the blessings to be bestowed in the kingdom. For this there was an Old Testament basis. The prophets had predicted that the law-giving function of Jehovah's kingship would enter upon a new stage in the Messianic age. According to Jeremiah God will then write his law upon the hearts of the people (Jer 31:33). According to Ezekiel he will make Israel to walk in his statutes (Ezek 36:27). The prophecies in the second part of Isaiah's book promise an impartation of righteousness to the people of God as a result of a new marvelous disclosure of Jehovah's own righteousness in the future. Jesus, who derived so many evangelical ideas from the last-mentioned source, may have had these prophecies in mind, when in the Sermon on the Mount he spoke of such as hunger and thirst after righteousness (Isa 55:1). At any rate the other beatitudes show that the state of mind here described is a receptive rather than a productive one. The hungering and thirsting stand on a line with the poor and the meek, they are conscious of not possessing the desired good in themselves and look to God for supplying it. When they are satisfied, this is due not to their own effort but to an act of God. The same thought is indirectly expressed in the "seeking" of righteousness commanded in Matt 6:33. In the parable of the Pharisee and publican the term "justification" is applied to an acceptance of man by God not based on self-righteous works, but on penitence and trust in the divine mercy.

It would be historically unwarranted to read into these utterances the whole doctrine of the imputed righteousness of Christ. It was impossible for Jesus to develop this doctrine with any degree of explicitness, because it was to be based on his own atoning death, which still lay in the future. Our Lord speaks of a state of righteousness before God to be conferred as a part of the coming kingdom. How far this will be done by imputation, how far it will also be done by changing the heart and life of men so as to produce works which God will be able in principle to approve in his judgment, which of these two will be the basis of the other is not clearly explained. Our Lord's doctrine is the bud in which the two conceptions of a righteousness imputed and a righteousness embodied in the sanctified life of the believer still lie enclosed together. Still it should not be overlooked, that in more than one respect Jesus prepared the way for Paul by enunciating principles to which the latter's teaching could attach itself. He emphasized that in the pursuit of righteousness the satisfaction of God should be man's supreme concern. This, carried out to its ultimate consequences with reference to sinful man, could not but lead to the conception of a righteousness provided by God himself in the perfect life and atoning death of Christ. He also affirmed that the righteousness required of the disciples was of an infinitely higher kind than that possessed by the Scribes and Pharisees, something as new and unprecedented as the kingdom itself, and thus raised the problem as to how this unique standing before God was to be acquired. Still further, he gave to understand that this righteousness was attainable by the disciples only, so that it must be held to rest on a previous state of acceptance by God, determined by his fatherhood and grace.

The third representation connects the kingdom with righteousness practiced in this life as a reward. Here obviously the kingdom denotes not the kingship of God, but the entire complex of resulting blessings, and that as they will be bestowed in the last day. Thus in Matt 5:20, the possession of a righteousness exceeding that of the Scribes and Pharisees appears as a prerequisite for entering the kingdom. The same idea underlies the numerous passages that speak of a future reward. It has been asserted that Jesus retained this whole line of thought, because he had not fully emancipated himself from the fundamental error of Judaism, according to which everything in religion revolved around the ideas of merit and reward. The charge, if well-founded, would be a serious one, for the principle in question, far from appearing in isolated sayings only, pervades the entire teaching of Jesus. The disciple's life is depicted throughout as a labor in the vineyard, at the plow, in the harvest-field, in the household. Treasures can be laid up in heaven.

In order to solve this difficulty it is necessary sharply to distinguish. The first thing to remember is that we have no right to declare the desire for reward as a motive in ethical conduct unworthy of a high standard of morality and therefore unworthy of the better element in our Lord's own teaching. This would be the case only, if it figured as the only or the supreme motive, and if other motives of a disinterested God-centered kind did not exist side by side with or above it. If our Lord appealed to the fear of punishment as a deterrent from evil, why should he not have appealed to the desire for blessedness and reward as an incentive to the good? May we not believe that Jesus himself was strengthened in enduring his suffering by the prospect of the promised glory (cf. Heb 12:2)? Does anybody think that in his case this interfered in the least with his making it his meat and his drink to do the Father's will?

Secondly, it should be emphasized that the stimulus afforded by the promise of reward need not appeal to the lower, sensual instincts, as but too often it did in the Jewish mind, but may equally well address itself to the highest, spiritual desires. In this respect our Lord's teaching moves on the highest conceivable plane. The pure in heart shall see God, those that hunger and thirst after righteousness shall be completely satisfied with the same, the peacemakers shall be called sons of God. These second clauses in the beatitudes describe the essence of the final kingdom in which the reward will consist. They show, therefore, that the reward towards which Jesus points his followers is not something morally or spiritually indifferent, but the highest enjoyment of what here already constitutes the natural blessedness pertaining to the internal kingdom. Thus the reward bears an organic relation to the conduct it is intended to crown.

Still further, we must observe that there is a fundamental difference between the manner in which Judaism conceived of the principle of reward and Jesus' conception of the same as regards the necessity with which this principle was believed to operate. According to the Jews this was a legal necessity; the fulfilment of the law being inherently worthy of and entitled to the reward following it. Hence also there existed between the two a ratio of strict equivalence, so much being given for so much. Jesus plainly taught that between God and man no such commercial relation can exist, not merely because this is impossible on account of man's sin, but for the deeper reason, that God's absolute sovereignty precludes it even under the conditions of human rectitude, because God as God is entitled, apart from every contract or stipulation of reward, to all the service or obedience man can render. The disciples are "unprofitable servants," even after they have done everything required of them (Luke 17:10). They are "unprofitable" not in the sense that their labors are useless, but in the sense that they can do no more for God their owner, than he can naturally expect of them. In the parable, the talents, for the increase of which the servants are rewarded, are not originally their own but entrusted to them by their Lord. As a result the relation of pure equivalence between what is done and what is received is entirely abolished. The reward will far exceed the righteousness which precedes it. He that is faithful over a few things will be set over many things, nay over all things (Matt 24:47; 25:21, 23). He who receives a prophet or a righteous man obtains a reward as great as that of the prophet and the righteous men (Matt 10:41–42). Restitution will be a hundredfold for things given up (Mark 10:30). And the parable of the laborers in the vineyard teaches that in its ultimate analysis the reward is a free gift, whence also the one who has labored but a little while can receive the full wages (Matt 20:1–16; cf. Luke 17:10).

We see, therefore, that Jesus, though giving a large place to the idea of reward in his teaching, keeps this idea in strict subordination to the two higher principles of the divine sovereignty and the divine grace, in other words to the divine kingship and the divine fatherhood. In the latter respect as well as in the former the relation between God and the disciples does not admit of the giving or receiving of rewards on the strictly commercial basis. The Father, as Father, gives to the little flock the kingdom, and in general bestows good gifts upon his children. What can be called wages from one point of view is a gracious gift from another (cf. Matt 5:46 with Luke 6:32, 35). The reward serves simply the purpose of affording an incentive to the disciples' zeal. Though the kingdom itself is inherited by all, and inherited by grace, there will be individual degrees in the glory which it involves for each disciple, because the ultimate issue cannot but be determined by the progress in righteousness made here below.

CHAPTER 8

THE ESSENCE OF THE KINGDOM CONTINUED:

THE KINGDOM AS A STATE OF BLESSEDNESS

We have already seen, that not the thought of man's welfare, but that of the glory of God was supreme in our Lord's teaching concerning the kingdom. While emphasizing this, we must not forget, however, that to him this thought was inseparably connected with the idea of the greatest conceivable blessedness for man. That God should reign was in his view so much the only natural, normal state of things, that he could not conceive of any true happiness apart from it, nor of it without a concomitant state of happiness for those who give to God the first and the highest place. This is in general the connection between the kingship of God as a rule over man, and the kingdom of God as a possession for man, a connection not obscurely indicated in the saying in Matt 6:33. With the kingship of God all other things must come, for, as Paul later expressed it: "If God be for us, who shall be against us?"

That this thought is not more frequently and more directly formulated admits of easy explanation. In deriving the state of blessedness from the character and will of God it was so natural to think of the divine fatherhood as its source, that the reference to God's kingship would scarcely suggest itself. Accordingly we find that the kingdom as a state of blessedness is represented as the Father's gift to the little flock rather than that of the King (Luke 12:32; cf. also Matt 20:32). It was quite possible, however, to reach the idea of blessedness by way of direct inference from that of the divine kingship. The Oriental king often bestows with royal munificence all manner of gifts upon his subjects. Illustrations of this both from sacred and other history will easily occur. Thus Jesus also speaks of the kingdom under the figure of a banquet prepared by the king as a marriage feast for his son (Matt 22:2). Nor should it be forgotten that the kingdom had been for Israel the instrument of gracious help in times of distress and a source of great national prosperity. The kingship had been in its ideal intent, and to some extent, at least in its better days, also in effect a democratic institution, to which the poor and the oppressed and miserable looked for aid and protection. There was therefore an easy transition from the idea of kingship to that of grace and salvation.

The inestimable value of the kingdom from man's point of view finds clearest expression in the parable of the treasure in the field and the pearl of great price. In both cases it is emphasized that the finder sells all his possessions in order to secure this one transcendent good (cf. Matt 19:12; Mark 9:43–47; Luke 18:29). That God himself regards the kingdom in this light appears from the fact of his having prepared it for his own from eternity (Matt 25:34). The preparation from eternity shows, that the kingdom is the supreme embodiment of the divine gracious purpose. Hence also the kingdom is said to be "inherited." Because the kingdom thus includes all that is truly valuable and precious, our Lord in connection with the kingdom-parables pronounces the disciples blessed who see and hear the truth concerning it. In doing this they are brought into immediate contact with the fulfilment of all the Old Testament promises. What many prophets and righteous men in vain desired to see and hear, is theirs in actual possession (Matt 13:16–17).

Looked at concretely, the blessings in which the kingdom consists are partly negative, partly positive in character. Negatively, the kingdom includes the deliverance from all evil. Foremost among the blessings pertaining to this side stands the forgiveness of sins. Prophecy had already spoken of this as an important element in the blessedness of the Messianic age (Jer 31:34). That Jesus considered this not merely as a preparation for the kingdom, but counted it of the very substance of the same may be seen from Matt 18:23ff., where the kingdom of heaven is likened unto a certain king, who graciously forgives the debt of his servant and releases him. Hence also the sequence in the Lord's Prayer, where the petition for the coming of the kingdom is followed first by that for the accomplishment of the will of God and next by that for the forgiveness of debts. Positively there corresponds to this the gift of righteousness, which cannot but carry with itself a sense of the highest spiritual delight and satisfaction for those who obtain it. The mind relieved from the burden of sin and assured of the divine acceptance enters upon a state of profound peace and rest (Matt 11:28–29; Mark 5:34; Luke 7:50).

The positive side of the blessedness received in the kingdom is chiefly described in the two important conceptions of sonship and of life. On these, therefore, we must briefly dwell at this point. While the two attributes of kingship and fatherhood mark two distinct elements in Jesus' conception of God, he certainly did not place them wide apart, much less regard them as intrinsically opposed to each other. The ease with which he passes over from the one to the other, e.g., in the opening words of the Lord's Prayer, shows that to his mind the two are perfectly harmonious attributes of the divine nature. There is a sense in which the effects of God's fatherhood can be subsumed under the kingdom-idea. As on the one hand the kingship might frequently originate through extension of the patriarchal authority beyond the limits of the tribe, so on the other hand the king could continue to sustain the relation of a father to his people. In point of fact the Old Testament represents Jehovah as by one and the same act becoming Israel's King and Israel's Father, viz., by the deliverance of the exodus (Exod 4:22; Deut 32:6; Isa 43:15).

That the place which belongs to sonship as one of the blessings of the kingdom is not always recognized with sufficient clearness finds its explanation in a widely current misunderstanding of our Lord's teaching on sonship. He is frequently interpreted as teaching the indiscriminate sonship of all men. Sonship then would be something which did not in any sense originate with the redemptive relation to God or with the kingdom of God. It is easy here to go to an extreme as well in absolutely denying as in indiscriminately affirming that our Lord made men the sons of God by nature. Some of his utterances, like the parable of the prodigal son, plainly imply that notwithstanding the sinner's estrangement from God a filial relationship continues to exist. The whole trend of his teaching is that redemption restores what has been disturbed by sin. But, granting this, we must not overlook two important considerations which would inevitably lead him to emphasize the newness of the sonship which is enjoyed in the redemptive state. On the one hand, Jesus had too profound a knowledge of the seriousness of sin not to recognize that it must render man unworthy and incapable of sonship in the full, original sense. On the other hand, he had also too high a conception of the transcendent perfection of the kingdom not to find in it in this respect as well as in others something that would far surpass any religious privilege that man could call his own by nature. The kingdom neutralizes the effects of sin, but it does far more than this. It carries man to the highest limit of knowledge and love and service and enjoyment of God of which he is capable, and nothing less than the attainment of this our Lord associates with the term "sonship." The words recorded in Luke 20:36, "They are equal unto the angels; and are sons of God, being sons of the resurrection," suffice to show that sonship to God appeared to him as the acme rather than as the common level of religious privilege (cf. also Matt 5:9).

And not only the sonship of man, but even the fatherhood of God admits of this high and exclusive application. For Jesus constantly speaks to the disciples of "your Father" (Matt 6:32). "*The* Father" in the Synoptical Gospels always denotes God in relation to "the Son," i.e., Jesus specifically. In the Fourth Gospel, where "*The* Father" is also used with reference to the disciples generally, this is not based on a conception of universal fatherhood, but on the thought that the relation originally existing between God and Jesus is extended to the disciples likewise. This, therefore, is the most emphatic assertion of the unique value of sonship. And this value was not confined in our Lord's estimation to the moral sphere, as one-sided modern representations sometimes make out. Sonship involves more than moral likeness to God, although this is of course one of its chief elements. Its rich religious meaning may be best perceived from the jubilant words in which Jesus speaks of his own filial relation to the Father (Matt 11:27), which, while unique in one sense, must yet bear a general resemblance to the sonship of the disciples. The most perfect mutual knowledge, the most direct communion of life, the most absolute unity of purpose, the joint possession of consummate blessedness and peace between God and man, all this forms part of the sonship in which the kingdom consists. The highest gift that can be bestowed on the pure in heart is that in the final kingdom they shall have the beatific filial vision of God face to face.

The second comprehensive term by which Jesus describes the blessedness of the kingdom is that of life. The Old Testament idea of life has for its prominent characteristics not so much the elements of growth and activity but rather those of prosperity and happiness in the possession of the favor of God. To this our Lord in his Synoptical teaching in the main adheres; only, in harmony with the prevailing Jewish usage, he projects the idea into the future, life being here equivalent to the sum total of the blessings and enjoyments of the final kingdom. Still even in the Synoptical teaching we find life occasionally spoken of as a present religious possession, and, therefore, as in its very essence a spiritual state (Matt 8:22; Luke 15:24, 32; 20:38). A present kingdom necessarily carries with itself a present enjoyment of life. And in the same degree as this is the case life also tends to become a life in the subjective sense of the word, a name for the believer's spiritual growth and activity, something to be "lived" as well as "inherited." In the discourses of the Fourth Gospel we can clearly observe how our Lord develops the idea in these two directions. His classical definition of life is found in the so-called high-priestly prayer: to know the only true God, and him whom he did send, even Jesus Christ (John 17:3). The knowledge of God here spoken of is, of course, something which in principle is already imparted in the present, although its consummate possession still lies in the future. It is a knowledge which is far more than mere intellectual cognition: it includes that practical acquaintance, that affectionate apprehension, which arise from congeniality of nature and the highest spiritual love. Hence what introduces into it is not a process of instruction, but a birth from above, or a re-birth, whereby the fundamental character is changed, so that from flesh, which naturally lives for this lower, earthly, sensual world, it becomes spirit, which naturally lives for the world of heaven and for God. Because Jesus is the personal representative and embodiment of this heavenly life on earth, he is the way unto God (John 14:6).

We see, therefore, how thoroughly this life, which constitutes man's blessed possession of the kingdom, is dominated by the thought of communion with God, as its chief source of enjoyment. In principle, however, the same thing is implied in some of the Synoptical sayings cited above, which approach the conception of life as something to be developed in man. When the prodigal in his hunger remembers the riches of his Father's house, he is said to have "come to himself." His return to the Father is described as a change from death into life: "This thy brother was dead, and is alive again, and was lost and is found" (Luke 15:32). Thus the re- adoption to sonship and the restoration to life are seen to coincide. If Jesus found in both the essence of the kingdom-privilege and kingdom-blessedness, which can be enjoyed on earth, we cannot doubt, that he also regarded them as supreme among the treasures and delights of the final kingdom. As the point of departure for his kingdom-conception lay in God, in the active exercise of God's royal sway, so its point of arrival lies in God, in God's gift of himself to man for everlasting possession. It is the teaching of Jesus, as well as of Paul, that from God and through God and unto God are all things.

CHAPTER 9

THE KINGDOM AND THE CHURCH

The conception of the kingdom is common to all periods of our Lord's teaching; that of the church emerges only at two special points of his ministry as recorded in Matt 16:18 and 18:17. The second of these two passages refers to the church quite incidentally, and, even if it speaks of the Christian church and not, as some have thought, of the Jewish ecclesiastical organization, throws no further light on the conception. The first on the other hand deals with the church for the express purpose of introducing it as something new, of describing its character and defining its relation to the kingdom. We are fortunate in having so explicit a statement of our Lord on this important matter. The subject should, of course, be approached historically. We must ask ourselves what there was in the situation of that particular juncture of our Lord's ministry that will account for this solitary and significant declaration about the church. Simon Peter had just made his important confession, "Thou art the Christ, the Son of the living God" (Matt 16:16). Our Lord thereupon announces that upon Peter, as the first confessor of his Messiahship in the face of the unbelief of the majority of the people, he will build his church, his ecclesia. The supposition is not that Peter has here for the first time reached this conviction regarding the Messianic dignity of Jesus, nor even that here for the first time utterance was given to such conviction. Unless we must disbelieve all our Gospels, both had taken place on earlier occasions. But the momentous significance of the present confession lay in this, that it was made at a juncture where many, who had previously followed Jesus, had forsaken him. It is the rock- character, the steadfastness of Peter that is praised by Jesus, that, when others wavered, he had remained true to his conviction. The revelation he had received from the Father in heaven was not the first disclosure of Jesus' Messiahship, but a revelation which enabled him, in distinction from the multitude, to discern in Jesus the true attributes of Messiahship, notwithstanding the outward appearance to the contrary.

Peter's confession, therefore, was distinctly a confession which stood in contrast with the rejection of Jesus by others. From this we may gather, that the church of which Jesus speaks will have for its peculiarity the recognition of the Messiahship of Jesus in contradistinction from the denial of this Messiahship by those without. But this follows not only from the situation in which the words were spoken, we may also draw the same conclusion from the tenor of the words themselves. When Jesus says "I will build *my* church," he evidently places this church over against another, to which this designation does not apply. The word *ecclesia* (ἐκκλησία) is the rendering of the Hebrew words *qahal* (קָהָל) and *ʿēdah* (עֵדָה), which latter were the standing names for the congregation of Israel. In such a connection "my church" can mean nothing else than "the church which by recognizing me as Messiah will take the place of the present Jewish church."

It would be a mistake, however, to suppose that the new church will rest exclusively on a subjective belief regarding the Messiahship of Jesus. Our Lord says emphatically "I will build," and thereby appropriates for himself the objective task of calling this church into existence by his Messianic acts. Though Peter confessing be the foundation, the church is not of Peter's or of any human making, the Lord himself will build it. And not only this, he will supremely rule in it, for out of the fullness of his authority he immediately proceeds to invest Peter with the power of the keys: "I will *give* unto thee" (Matt 16:19). Objectively considered, therefore, the church is that new congregation taking the place of the old congregation of Israel, which is formed by Jesus as the Messiah and stands under his Messianic rule.

Even this, however, does not fully exhaust the import of our Lord's statement. It will be noticed, that he refers both the building of the church and the exercise of his authority with regard to it to the future: "I *will* build" and "I *will* give." At the present time of speaking the church is not yet; if its origin and government depend on the Messiahship of Jesus, then clearly this Messiahship must here be taken in a specific sense, the realization of which also still lay in the future. Our Lord can refer to nothing else than the new exalted, heavenly state upon which his person and work would enter through his death and resurrection and seating at the right hand of God. In order to understand this we must remember that Jesus, while in one sense conscious of having Messianic authority and doing

Messianic work already here on earth, yet in another sense regarded the exercise of his Messianic function as beginning with his state of glory. It was entirely in harmony with Jesus' own point of view when Peter later declared that God by the resurrection had *made* him both Lord and Christ (Acts 2:36). Now in this sense we can say that according to our Lord's teaching the church could not begin until after he should have entered upon the exalted stage of his Messiahship. That Jesus' speaking in terms of the future has reference to this and nothing else, may also be gathered from the following fact: The Evangelist tells us that from that announcement concerning the church onward, Jesus began to show unto his disciples that he must go unto Jerusalem, and suffer many things of the elders and chief priests and scribes, and be killed, and the third day be raised up (Matt 16:21). Plainly then in his mind there was a connection between the results of his suffering and the origin of the church.

So far we have considered our Lord's words exclusively in their reference to the church and not inquired into their bearing upon the doctrine of the kingdom. We now observe, that the church, here for the first time formally introduced, is most closely related to the kingdom, which had hitherto occupied the foremost place in Jesus' teaching. For immediately after the declaration concerning the building of the church, our Lord continues to say unto Peter: "I will give unto thee the keys of the kingdom of heaven; and whatsoever thou shalt bind on earth shall be bound in heaven; and whatsoever thou shalt loose on earth shall be loosed in heaven" (Matt 16:19). It would not be impossible, of course, to give a plausible interpretation of this connection on the view, that the church and the kingdom are separate things. Understanding the kingdom as the final kingdom, and the power of the keys as the power to give or deny entrance, the sense might be that to Peter, as the foundation of the church, and therefore to the church, had been given the power in some way or other to open or shut the gates of the heavenly kingdom. On this view the church would be distinct from the kingdom as here spoken of, would indeed stand related to it as a gate-keeper stands to a house. This is, however, scarcely a possible exegesis so far as the words of the second declaration themselves are concerned. The binding and loosing do not refer to heaven itself, as if heaven were shut or opened, but refer to certain things lying within the sphere of heaven, and not of heaven alone but of earth likewise.

The figure of binding and loosing will have to be understood in a different sense. We have the choice between interpreting it of the binding and loosing of sin, i.e. the imputation and forgiveness of sin, and interpreting it as an instance of the common Jewish parlance which employed "to bind" in the sense of "to forbid," "to loose" in the sense of "to allow." The former might seem to be favored by Matt 18:18, where the same expressions occur and the connection leads us to think of the process of church discipline. In Matt 16, on the other hand, there is nothing to indicate that the figure has this restricted sense, on the contrary, everything points to the most generalizing interpretation that can be put upon it. The keys spoken of are in all probability not the keys of the outer door, but the keys pertaining to the entire house, the keys not of the gate-keeper, but of the house-steward, and therefore symbolize the administration of the affairs of the house in general (cf. Isa 22:22; Rev 3:7). But, whichever of these two last mentioned views we may adopt, in either case the kingdom of heaven appears as something existing, in part at least, on earth. Peter receives the keys of the kingdom to bind or loose on earth. What he does in the administration of the kingdom here below will be recognized in heaven. Now this promise immediately following the declaration concerning Peter as the foundation rock of the church, it becomes necessary to assume that in Jesus' view these two are identified. The force of this will be felt by observing that in the two statements made the figure is essentially the same, viz., that of the house. First the house is represented as in process of building, and Peter as the foundation, then the same house appears as completed and Peter as invested with the keys for administering its affairs. It is plainly excluded that the house should mean one thing in the first statement and another in the second. It must be possible, this much we may confidently affirm, to call the church the kingdom. It is another question, to which we shall presently revert, whether the kingdom can under all circumstances be identified with the church.

The kingdom as the church bears the features of a community of men. It appears as a house. This character belonged to the Old Testament church for which that of Jesus is substituted, it also finds expression in the very name *ecclesia* (ἐκκλησία) which designates the assembly of free citizens called together to deliberate and take action in matters pertaining to the commonwealth. There are traces in Jesus' earlier teaching of his having viewed the kingdom under this aspect as an organism of men, although the representation is by no means prominent. Sayings like Matt 20:25; Mark 9:35; Luke 20:25, at least suggest the idea of the kingdom as a society based on a totally different principle from that governing the kingdoms of this world. In point of fact, Jesus gathered around himself a company of disciples, and it is plausible to assume that he found in their mutual association the beginning of what the kingdom of God was from its very nature intended to be. The two parables of the wheat and the tares and of the fish-net equally imply the thought that the kingdom is an aggregate of men, though their point does not lie in this thought as such, but in the inevitable intermingling of the good and bad until the end. The nearest approach to the later declaration about the church occurs in the expression "his kingdom" of Matt 13:41. This "kingdom of the Son of man" agrees with the "church of Jesus," in that both phrases make the kingdom a body of men placed under the Messiah as their ruler.

From the foregoing it appears, that, if the church represents an advance beyond the internal, invisible kingdom, which had hitherto figured so largely in our Lord's teaching, the advance must be sought in something else than the mere fact of its being a body of disciples. The advance lies in two points. In the first place, the body of disciples previously existing must now take the place of the Old Testament church and therefore receive some form of external organization. This the kingdom had not hitherto possessed. It had been internal and invisible not merely in its essence, but to this essence there had been lacking the outward embodiment. Jesus now in speaking of the house and the keys of the house, of binding and loosing on earth, and of church discipline, makes provision for this. In the second place, our Lord gives to understand that the new stage upon which his Messiahship is now about to enter, will bring to the kingdom a new influx of supernatural power and thus make out of it, not only externally but also internally, that new thing which he calls his church.

It is possible to find this referred to in the words about the gates of Hades, which immediately follow the Lord's declaration that he will build his church. According to some, these words imply a conflict between Hades as the realm of death and the church as the sphere of life. They then would mean that death will not be able to conquer the church, or that the church will be able to conquer death, and the ground for this promise would be that Jesus will soon win a victory over death and fill his church with unconquerable life (Rev 1:18). Probably, however, the correct rendering is "the gates of Hades shall not surpass it." The gates of Hades seem to have been a figure for the highest conceivable strength, because no one can break through them. On this rendering our Lord simply means to say that the church will not be excelled in strength by the strongest that is known; the figure is a further elaboration of the idea that the church is built upon a rock. There are, however, other sayings belonging to the same closing period of our Lord's ministry, in which he predicts the coming of the kingdom with a new, previously unknown power. In Matt 16:28; Mark 9:1; Luke 9:27; Matt 26:64; Mark 14:62; Luke 22:69, Jesus speaks of a coming of the Son of man in his kingdom, of a coming of the kingdom of God with power, which will take place in the near future, so that some of the people then living will witness it. A common way of interpreting these sayings is to refer them to the final coming of the kingdom at the end of the world. Those, however, who adopt this view, must assume that our Lord was mistaken as to the nearness of the event in question and hence give up the infallibility of his teaching.

Another exegesis is quite possible. We can interpret these sayings of the coming of the kingdom in the church. The strong terms in which they are clothed do not absolutely forbid this. It must be acknowledged that these terms resemble the language in which elsewhere the final coming of the kingdom is spoken of. It is a coming of the kingdom with power, a coming of Jesus in his kingdom, even a coming of Jesus with the clouds of heaven. But these expressions become more easily explainable, if we endeavor to realize what the church in her first appearance was to be, and how the immediate future presented itself to Jesus from his own personal point of view. In the early church there were to be many extraordinary manifestations of the Spirit's power, so extraordinary indeed as to anticipate in some respects the phenomena that will be observed at the end of the world. And, even apart from this, the presence of the Spirit in the church in its more ordinary form of operation is something sufficiently marvelous and stupendous to justify the strong terms employed. The church actually has within herself the powers of the world to come. She is more than the immanent kingdom as it existed before Jesus' exaltation. She forms an intermediate link between the present life and the life of eternity. Here we can best observe how thoroughly supernaturalistic our Lord's conception of the church-form of the kingdom is. And our Lord looked upon the appearance of this church from a point of view that was peculiarly his own. He was to be its Lord and King. Now to him there was not that sharp division between the church-kingdom and the final kingdom which there is for us who live on earth. For him the consummation of the kingdom in which all is fulfilled began with his resurrection and ascension. It is therefore not unnatural that he should speak of this approaching state in terms which, in themselves considered, might make us think of the final coming of the kingdom.

Besides these passages we have the statement of Matt 18:20, in which our Lord promises to be present in the midst of his disciples in a peculiar manner, and which throws light upon the idea of a coming of his which shall precede the final coming. But especially do the Saviour's last discourses preserved for us in the Gospel according to John afford us help in apprehending his meaning on this point. Here he plainly represents himself as coming to the disciples in the Spirit, and that in a way quite distinct from the manner in which he will come at the end of the world. It is a coming which the disciples will witness, whilst to others he will not reveal himself. It cannot be said to refer to the bodily appearances of Jesus after the resurrection, for it is intended to result in an abiding presence. Here, therefore, we have something quite analogous to the Synoptical statements previously quoted, the only difference being that the conception of the kingdom itself is wanting here as elsewhere in John.

From what has been said it appears that every view which would keep the kingdom and the church separate as two entirely distinct spheres is not in harmony with the trend of our Lord's teaching. The church is a form which the kingdom assumes in result of the new stage upon which the Messiahship of Jesus enters with his death and resurrection. So far as extent of membership is concerned, Jesus plainly leads us to identify the invisible church and the kingdom. It is impossible to be in the one without being in the other. We have our Lord's explicit declaration in John 3:3, 5, to the effect that nothing less than the new birth can enable man to see the kingdom or enter into it. The kingdom, therefore, as truly as the invisible church is constituted by the regenerate; the regenerate alone experience in themselves its power, cultivate its righteousness, enjoy its blessings. It is, of course, quite possible, while recognizing this identity of extent, to make distinctions as to the point of view from which the regenerate are called the kingdom and the church. Various attempts in this direction have been made. It may be said that the kingdom designates believers in their relation to God as ruler, the church believers in their separateness from the world and their organic union with one another. Or, that the church designates believers in their attitude of worship towards God, the kingdom, believers in their ethical activities towards one another. Or again, that the church designates the people of God from the point of view of their calling to be God's instrument in preparing the way for and introducing the ideal order of things, the kingdom, the same people of God so far as they possess the ideal order in principle realized among themselves. These and similar distinctions have their doctrinal usefulness and are unobjectionable, so long as they do not obscure the fact that the kingdom, as well as the church, is circumscribed by the line of regeneration, and that the invisible church itself is that which determines its inner essence, its relation to God and Christ, a true kingdom, since it consists of those over whom the Messiah rules as the representative of God.

But what about the relation of the visible church to the kingdom? Here again we must first of all insist upon it, that our Lord looked upon the visible church as a veritable embodiment of his kingdom. Precisely because the invisible church realizes the kingship of God, the visible church must likewise partake of this character. We have seen that the power of binding and loosing given to the church is described under the figure of the keys of the kingdom of heaven. Our Lord in conferring this power acts in the capacity of King over the visible church. In Matt 13:41 the kingdom of the Son of man, out of which the angels in the last day will remove all things that cause stumbling and them that do iniquity, is nothing else but the visible church. The visible church is constituted by the enthronement of Christ as the King of glory. Out of the fullness of his royal authority he gave immediately before ascending the great commission to preach the gospel and disciple the nations and instituted the sacrament of baptism. We must say, therefore, that the kingdom-forces which are at work, the kingdom-life which exists in the invisible sphere, find expression in the kingdom-organism of the visible church. That Christ is King in this church and all authority exercised within any church-body derives from him is an important principle of church government, which those who endeavor to distinguish between the kingdom of God and the visible church do not always sufficiently keep in mind.

From this, however, it does not necessarily follow, that the visible church is the only outward expression of the invisible kingdom. Undoubtedly the kingship of God, as his recognized and applied supremacy, is intended to pervade and control the whole of human life in all its forms of existence. This the parable of the leaven plainly teaches. These various forms of human life have each their own sphere in which they work and embody themselves. There is a sphere of science, a sphere of art, a sphere of the family and of the state, a sphere of commerce and industry. Whenever one of these spheres comes under the controlling influence of the principle of the divine supremacy and glory, and this outwardly reveals itself, there we can truly say that the kingdom of God has become manifest. Now our Lord in his teaching seldom makes explicit reference to these things. He contented himself with laying down the great religious and moral principles which ought to govern the life of man in every sphere. Their detailed application it was not his work to show. But we may safely affirm two things. On the one hand, his doctrine of the kingdom was founded on such a profound and broad conviction of the absolute supremacy of God in all things, that he could not but look upon every normal and legitimate province of human life as intended to form part of God's kingdom. On the other hand, it was not his intention that this result should be reached by making human life in all its spheres subject to the visible church. It is true that under the Old Covenant something of this nature had existed. In the theocracy the church had dominated the life of the people of

God in all its extent. State and church were in it most intimately united. Jesus on more than one occasion gave to understand that in this respect at least the conditions of the Old Covenant were not to be perpetuated (cf. Matt 22:21; John 18:36; 19:11). And what is true of the relation between church and state, may also be applied to the relation between the visible church and the various other branches into which the organic life of humanity divides itself. It is entirely in accordance with the spirit of Jesus' teaching to subsume these under the kingdom of God and to co-ordinate them with the visible church as true manifestations of this kingdom, in so far as the divine sovereignty and glory have become in them the controlling principle. But it must always be remembered, that the latter can only happen, when all these, no less than the visible church, stand in living contact with the forces of regeneration supernaturally introduced into the world by the Spirit of God. While it is proper to separate between the visible church and such things as the Christian state, Christian art, Christian science, etc., these things, if they truly belong to the kingdom of God, grow up out of the regenerated life of the invisible church.

As already stated, this is a subject on which our Lord's teaching does not bring any explicit disclosures and which can only be treated by way of inference. It has sometimes been thought that the parables of the wheat and the tares and of the fish-net contain an explicit declaration concerning the kingdom as a wider sphere than the church. This is assumed, because these parables imply that in the kingdom the good and the evil are to be allowed to intermingle, which cannot be the rule in the church, as the obligation to exercise church discipline plainly shows. Historically interpreted, however, these parables do not warrant such an inference. The current doctrine of the kingdom, shared up to that point by the disciples, assumed that the very first act of God at the coming of the kingdom would consist in an absolute and eternal separation between the good and the evil. This assumption was natural so long as no distinction between the two stages of the history of the kingdom had been made. When Jesus introduced this distinction, it became necessary to emphasize that not everything which was true of the final appearance of the kingdom could therefore also be predicated of its present, invisible mode of coming. As a warning to this effect these two parables must be interpreted.

Our Lord desires to make plain that, while the kingdom is now actually coming, a complete separation between the evil and the good cannot be effected until the end of the world. During the present age the kingdom must partake of the limitations and imperfections to which a sinful environment exposes it. Of the church, as the externally organized kingdom, this is eminently true. It exists upon the field of the world. At no time until the very last will it be entirely purified of all evil elements. This truth, however, in no wise interferes with the possibility nor absolves from the duty of church discipline. The process to which our Lord refers in Matt 18:17 is not intended for effecting an absolute separation between the good and the evil, and thus rendering the church as ideally pure as she will be in the final state of the kingdom. Its proximate end is the self-preservation of the church in that state of holiness which befits her profession, and would be destroyed by the exercise of religious fellowship with such as remain unrepentant in the face of open sin. Its ulterior end is remedial, consisting in the salvation of the sinner thus left to himself. Both ends can be pursued without forgetting or denying the lesson taught in the parables, that it is not given to men to judge the heart, and that God alone in the day of judgment will infallibly remove from the church all elements which, while simulating its outward appearance, do not belong to it in the inner spiritual reality.

CHAPTER 10

THE ENTRANCE INTO THE KINGDOM:

REPENTANCE AND FAITH

F rom the beginning our Lord's announcement of the
nearness of the kingdom was linked with the demand for
repentance and faith (Matt 4:17; Mark 1:15). This was not
accidental, but an inevitable result from the nature of the
kingdom. Repentance and faith are simply the two main
aspects of the kingdom, righteousness and the saving grace of
God, translated into terms of subjective human experience.
Because the kingdom is in its very essence a kingdom of
righteousness, therefore it is impossible for anyone to be truly
in it without having previously repented. Because the kingdom
intrinsically consists in the exercise of the divine saving grace
and power, therefore it requires in every one who is to share its
benefits that responsive and receptive attitude towards these
divine attributes which is called faith.

The relation of repentance to the kingdom is strikingly
defined in Matthew's version of the parable of the marriage
feast (Matt 22:1–14). Comparing this with the form in which our

Lord uttered the same parable on a previous occasion, according to Luke 14:16–24, we find among other changes the significant touch added of the man without a wedding garment. It is plain from the nature of the invitation, that what this wedding garment stands for is not to be regarded as in any way entitling the bearer to a place at the feast. Those who come are taken from the highways and hedges, from the streets and lanes of the city and compelled to enter. They are received, therefore, without merit on their part, on the principle of free grace. Nevertheless, when once within, it is indispensable that they should wear the garment appropriate to the occasion. Thus repentance and righteousness, while they do not in any meritorious sense earn the benefits of the kingdom, are yet indispensable concomitants of the state in which alone these benefits can be received.

Our Lord's idea of repentance is as profound and comprehensive as his conception of righteousness. Of the three words that are used in the Greek Gospels to describe the process, one emphasizes the emotional element of regret, sorrow over the past evil course of life, μεταμέλομαι (*metamelomai*; Matt 21:29–32); a second expresses reversal of the entire mental attitude, μετανοέω (*metanoeō*; Matt 12:41; Luke 11:32; 15:7, 10); the third denotes a change in the direction of life, one goal being substituted for another, ἐπιστρέφομαι (*epistrephomai*; Matt 13:15 and parallels; Luke 17:4; 22:32). Repentance is not limited to any single faculty of the mind: it engages the entire man, intellect, will and affections. Nor is it confined to the moral sphere of life in the narrower sense: it covers man's entire religious as well as his moral relation to God. Repentance in the conception of Jesus is wide enough to include faith (Matt 11:20–21). Here as elsewhere, what strikes us most is the God-centered character of our Lord's teaching on the subject. The state from which a repentance must take place is condemned, because it is radically wrong with reference to God. The sin of the prodigal has for its central feature the abandonment of the Father's house. The sinful are like wandering sheep, like lost coins, representations which imply a detachment of the spiritual consciousness from its center in God.

The strongest way of expressing this is to designate the state of man without repentance a state of death (Matt 8:22; Luke 15:24, 32. And Jesus does not look upon this state as a godless state in the purely negative sense of the word. Where the love of God is absent, there an idolatrous love of the world and of self enters, and a positively offensive and hostile attitude towards God results. It is very significant that Jesus, in speaking of the two masters, does not say that to love the one is to neglect the other, or to hold to the one is to renounce the other, but employs positive terms in both clauses, "Either he will hate the one and love the other, or else he will hold to the one and despise the other" (Matt 6:24). Man is so necessarily bound to God in his inmost consciousness, that absolute indifference or neutrality are excluded.

In the crisis of repentance the offense against God and the need of God are that upon which the repenting consciousness is focused. The sorrow of true repentance is one which arises from conviction of sin. It is also a sorrow after God, such as proceeds from a sense of spiritual destitution. Both principles are well brought out in the parable of the prodigal son, the discourse in which Jesus has so marvelously described the psychological process of repentance. The prodigal "comes to himself." Previously he had been out of himself, had not known and felt himself in the simple truth of his fundamental relation to God. He realizes that he perishes with hunger, whilst in his

Father's house there is bread enough and to spare. In his confession the offense against God is significantly placed before that against the human father.

Again, in the new life which follows repentance the absolute supremacy of God is the controlling principle. He who repents turns away from the service of mammon and self to the service of God. Our Lord is emphatic in insisting upon this absolute, undivided surrender of the soul to God as the goal of all true repentance. Because this and nothing less is the goal, he urges the necessity of a constant repetition of the process. Even to his followers he said at a comparatively late stage of his ministry, "Except ye turn and become as little children, ye shall in no wise enter into the kingdom of heaven" (Matt 18:3). From this necessity we must also explain the uncompromising manner in which Jesus requires of his disciples the renunciation of all earthly bonds and possessions which would dispute God his supreme sway over their life (Matt 10:39; 16:25; Luke 14:25–35). The statements to this effect are not meant in the sense that external abandonment of these things is sufficient or even required. The idea is that the inward attachment of the soul to them as the highest good must be in principle destroyed, that God may take the place hitherto claimed by them. Within the kingdom they are entitled to affection on the disciple's part in so far only as they can be made subordinate and subservient to the love of God. The demand for sacrifice always presupposes that what is to be renounced forms an obstacle to that absolute devotion which the kingdom of God requires (Mark 9:43). That not the external possession but the internal entanglement of the heart with temporal goods is condemned, Jesus strikingly indicates by the demand "to hate" one's father and mother and wife and children and brethren and sisters, yea and one's own life also. The energetic determination of the will to forego even the pleasures of natural affection, where they come in conflict with the supreme duty of the kingdom, is thus described and the word "hating" chosen on purpose to express that in such cases an internal change of mind alone, not a mere external act, can make man fit for the kingdom of God. Matthew 10:37 gives us Jesus' own interpretation of such seemingly harsh sayings.

Jesus affirms the necessity of repentance for all men (Mark 6:12; Luke 13:3, 5; 24:47). In an indirect way the universal need of it is shown by his utterances on the universality and pervasiveness of sin. Even to the disciples it can be said without qualification, "If ye then, being evil, etc." (Matt 7:11). None is good save one, even God (Mark 10:18). It is true Jesus draws a distinction between "righteous" and "sinners" (Matt 9:13; Mark 2:17). But the context shows that this distinction is drawn from the point of view of the judgment pronounced by men on themselves, not from the objective standpoint of Jesus' own knowledge of them. These statements were made in answer to the charge of the Pharisees that Jesus ate with publicans and sinners. The Saviour means to say that, if their comparative estimate concerning themselves and these degraded people be correct, there is all the more necessity for his associating with the latter in order to save them. Perhaps the reference to the ninety and nine righteous persons, which need no repentance, in Luke 15:7, 10, must be explained on the same principle.

The connection between faith and the saving grace and power of God in the kingdom is just as close and vital as that just traced between repentance and righteousness. It is a striking fact that in the Synoptical Gospels nearly the whole of our Lord's teaching on faith attaches itself to the performance of miracles. This implies that the miracles were eminently adapted to bring out the inner essence of faith and to reveal the true reason for its necessity. They embody that aspect of the kingdom to which faith is the subjective counterpart. Now the miracles almost without exception have two features in common. In the first place, they are transactions where the result absolutely and exclusively depends on the forth-putting of the divine supernatural power, where no human effort could possibly contribute anything towards its accomplishment. And secondly, the miracles are, as we have seen, healing miracles in which the gracious love of God offers itself to man for his salvation. Faith is the spiritual attitude called for by this twofold element in the saving work of God. It is the recognition of the divine power and grace, not, of course, in a purely intellectual way, but practically so as to involve not only conviction of the mind but to carry with it also the movement of the will and the affections. How faith stands related to the saving power of God is most clearly illustrated in the narrative Mark 9:17–24. When the disciples could not heal the child with the dumb spirit Jesus exclaimed, "O unbelieving generation." The father says, after describing the severity of the case, "But if thou canst do anything, have compassion on us and help us." To this Jesus replies, "If thou canst! all things are possible to him that believeth." This ascribes to faith something that can be affirmed of God alone, viz., absolute omnipotence. Elsewhere also this principle is emphasized by our Lord (Matt 21:21–22; Mark 11:22–23; Luke 17:6). The explanation lies in this that faith is nothing else than that act whereby man lays hold of, appropriates for himself the endless power of God. If faith were a human endeavor, something working by its own inherent strength, then it would be indeed reasonable to say with reference to the one exercising it, "If thou canst." On the other hand, if the innermost meaning of faith consist precisely in this, that man with an utter renunciation of his own strength, casts himself upon the strength of God, then plainly all further concern about what is possible or impossible, every "If thou canst," is out of place. Hence also faith is not a quantitative matter, as it would have to be, were it a principle of human endeavor; faith like a grain of mustard seed will accomplish the greatest conceivable results, because, small though it be, it nevertheless, provided it be genuine faith, connects man with the exhaustless reservoir of divine omnipotence (Luke 17:6).

This line of reasoning, however, is not applicable to the miracles only. The miracles illustrate the saving work of God in general. All salvation partakes, humanly speaking, of the nature of the impossible, can be accomplished by God alone. Jesus answers the question of the disciples, "Who then can be saved?" with an appeal to the almighty power of God, "With men this is impossible, but with God all things are possible" (Matt 19:25–26). All genuine saving faith is as profoundly conscious of its utter dependence on God for deliverance from sin as the recipients of our Lord's miraculous cures were convinced that God alone could heal their bodies from disease.

But faith is more than a conviction regarding the necessity and sufficiency of the divine power. It also involves the recognition of God's willingness and readiness to save, is a practical appropriation of the divine grace. Thus there enters into it an element of trust. Jesus never encouraged the exercise of faith as a mere external belief in supernatural power. The performance of a sign from heaven, which men might have witnessed without such trust in God or himself, he persistently refused. Where there existed an antecedent hindrance to the exercise of this trust, he would not even perform any healing miracles. He, who truly believes, vividly realizes that God is loving, merciful, forgiving, glad to receive sinners. Faith transfers to God what human parents experience in themselves with reference to their own children, the desire to help and supply (Matt 7:7–11). Not to trust would be to ascribe to him the evil disposition of sinful men towards one another. This reliance of faith is not confined to the critical moments of life, it is to be the abiding, characteristic inner disposition of the disciple with reference to every concern. To trust God for food and raiment is as truly the mark of the disciple in the kingdom as to depend on him for eternal salvation (Matt 6:30). Faith in those on whom the wonderful cures were wrought may have manifested itself at first as a momentary act, but Jesus frequently called the attention of such people to what faith had done for them, thus suggesting that this faith could be made fruitful also on future occasions. Of the disciples he explicitly required faith as an abiding disposition of trust. When in the storm they came to him saying, "Save Lord, we perish," he rebuked them because they were without confidence in his presence with them as a source of absolute safety.

Being in its very essence trust, faith necessarily rests in a person. It is not confidence about any abstract proposition, but reliance upon a personal character and disposition. The disciples are urged to have "faith in God" (Mark 11:22). But, inasmuch as Jesus is the revelation and representative of God, nay, one with God, he also is the personal object of faith. It is true, in the Synoptical Gospels this is explicitly stated in one passage only, viz., Matt 18:6, "These little ones that believe on me." But this almost entire absence of the formula is easily explained. It was the result of Jesus' method of not directly proclaiming at first his own position in the kingdom, but rather of allowing it to be gradually inferred from practical experience. It does not prove the assertion of some modern writers, that in the gospel, as Jesus preached it, there was no place for his own person, that it was merely a gospel about God. Though not frequently in so many words, yet in acts we find our Lord seeking to elicit and cultivate a personal relationship of faith between the disciple and himself and in himself with God. Conscious of being the Messiah, he could not help assigning to himself a place in the gospel, and viewing himself as in a real sense the object of religious trust. This appears from his saying to Peter shortly before the passion, "Simon, Simon, behold Satan asked to have you, that he might sift you (notice the plural pronoun) as wheat: but I made supplication for thee, that thy faith fail not." Here the crisis of our Lord's suffering is represented as the great testing crisis of true discipleship. Satan will in it sift the true disciples from the false. The true will approve themselves in this, that, when everything goes against Jesus, their faith fails not. And, on the other hand, when Peter's faith begins to fail, this is described as a denial of Jesus; faith, therefore, must involve the opposite of denial, an avowal, a personal bond of identification between the master and the disciple (Luke 22:31–34). And it is psychologically inconceivable that in those who were helped by the miracles of Jesus, faith should not have assumed the form of personal trust in him as the instrument of the saving grace and power of God. Faith in God and faith in Jesus here inevitably coalesced.

Faith is not represented by our Lord as an arbitrary movement of the mind, which would be independent of the deeper-lying dispositions and tendencies of life. Jesus knows of antecedent states of heart by which faith and unbelief are determined. The unbelief of the Jews he explains from the fact of their being "offended" in him. What Jesus was and did and taught stood at almost every point in direct antithesis to what they expected their Messiah to be, to do and to teach. But these expectations and beliefs of the Jews were deeply rooted in their general religious state and character: their unbelief, therefore, resulted from the fundamental disposition of their hearts. They that refuse faith do so, because they are an evil and adulterous generation. If they were what they ought to be and had not broken the pledges of their covenant marriage to God, if their attitude towards God were normal, they would believe on him whom God had sent. And all this is true likewise of faith. In its ultimate analysis faith is, according to Jesus, a divine gift. Faith must be the work of God in man, because only so can it be in harmony with itself as the recognition that we owe everything to God's working for us and in us. It is the Father who reveals to the babes what he hides from the wise and understanding (Matt 11:25). Jesus prays for Peter, that his faith fail not: that which we pray for we affirm to be dependent on the operation of God. When Peter makes his confession, "Thou art the Christ, the Son of the living God" (Matt 16:16), Jesus declares that not flesh and blood has revealed this unto him, but the Father in heaven.

In the discourses of the Gospel according to John, several important points of our Lord's doctrine of faith are brought out with greater clearness and explicitness than in the Synoptical statements. Faith here is from beginning to end faith in Jesus, and not merely in Jesus as the instrument of God, but as the image and incarnation of God, so that to believe in him is to believe in God. Consequently this faith in Jesus is also more clearly represented as a comprehensive faith in him as a Saviour for life and death, for time and eternity, and not merely faith in Jesus as helper in a concrete case of distress. Still further our Lord here by anticipation describes how faith will stand related to his atonement and resurrection, how it will become faith in the heavenly, glorified Christ (John 3:14; 6:51; 7:29, 38; 11:25; 15:7, 16; 16:23, 24). Because the testimony of Jesus concerning himself in this Gospel is so much fuller and richer, faith is more closely identified with knowledge (John 6:69; 8:24, 28; 14:9–10, 20; 16:30). We have already seen above, however, that knowledge here means far more than intellectual cognition. It implies practical acquaintance, confidence and love (John 10:4, 14–15; 17:25–26). Finally, our Lord is here much more explicit on the causes of faith and unbelief than in the more popular Synoptical teaching. Faith and unbelief are experimental states and acts in which the whole spiritual condition of the individual comes to light. Not to believe is the great sin, because the deep inherent sinfulness of the heart displays in this sin its true character of hostility towards God (John 9:41; 15:22, 24; 16:8–9). In the same manner faith is the outcome of an inward condition of the heart. This our Lord describes as a doing of the truth, a working in God, a being of the truth, a having of the love of God in one's self, a hearing from the Father, a learning from him, a being drawn by the Father, a having been given by the Father to the Son, in virtue of which believers are Jesus' own sheep even before he manifests himself to them (John 3:21; 5:42; 6:44–45; 17:11; 18:37). In all these respects the teaching of Jesus here recorded is not in contradiction with, but simply the legitimate expansion of that delivered to us in the three other Gospels.

CHAPTER 11

RECAPITULATION

Having reached the end of our discussion we may now endeavor briefly to formulate the important principles embodied in our Lord's teaching on the Kingdom of God and the Church. They are the following:

In the first place, the kingdom-conception involves the historic unity of Jesus' work with the Old Testament work of God. These two constitute one body of supernatural revelation and redemption.

Secondly, the doctrine of the kingdom stands for the principle that the Christian religion is not a mere matter of subjective ideas or experiences, but is related to a great system of objective, supernatural facts and transactions. The kingdom means the renewal of the world through the introduction of supernatural forces.

Thirdly, the kingdom-idea is the clearest expression of the principle that in the sphere of objective reality, as well as in the sphere of human consciousness, everything is subservient to the glory of God. In this respect the kingdom is the most profoundly religious of all biblical conceptions.

Fourthly, the message of the kingdom imparts to Christianity, as Jesus proclaims it, the professed character of a religion of salvation, and of salvation not primarily by man's own efforts but by the power and grace of God. The kingdom represents the specifically evangelical element in our Lord's teaching. The same principle finds subjective expression in his teaching on faith.

Fifthly, Jesus' doctrine of the kingdom as both inward and outward, coming first in the heart of man and afterwards in the external world, upholds the primacy of the spiritual and ethical over the physical. The invisible world of the inner religious life, the righteousness of the disposition, the sonship of God are in it made supreme, the essence of the kingdom, the ultimate realities to which everything else is subordinate. The inherently ethical character of the kingdom finds subjective expression in the demand for repentance.

Sixthly, that form which the kingdom assumes in the church shows it to be inseparably associated with the person and work of Jesus himself. The religion of the kingdom is a religion in which there is not only a place but in which the central place is for the Saviour. The church form of the kingdom rightly bears the name of Christianity, because in it on Christ everything depends.

Finally, the thought of the kingdom of God implies the subjection of the entire range of human life in all its forms and spheres to the ends of religion. The kingdom reminds us of *the absoluteness, the pervasiveness, the unrestricted dominion,* which of right belong to all true religion. It proclaims that religion, and religion alone, can act as *the supreme unifying, centralizing factor* in the life of man, as that which binds all together and perfects all by leading it to its final goal in the service of God.

THE END.

SCRIPTURE INDEX

Old Testament

New Testament